Aspects of modern sociology

The social structure of modern Britain

GENERAL EDITORS

John Barron Mays
Eleanor Rathbone Professor of Sociology, University of Liverpool

Maurice Craft
Goldsmiths' Professor of Education, University of London

The Working Class

Kenneth Roberts, B.Sc. (Soc.), M.Sc. (Econ.)

Lecturer in Sociology
University of Liverpool

Longman
London and New York

Longman Group Limited London

Associated companies, branches and representatives throughout the world

Published in the United States of America by Longman Inc., New York

First published 1978

Library of Congress Cataloging in Publication Data

Roberts, Kenneth, 1940–
    The working class.

    (Aspects of modern sociology)
    Bibliography: p.
    Includes index.
    1. Labor and laboring classes—Great Britain.
    2. Great Britain—Social conditions—1945–
    I. Title.
HD8383.5.R62   301.44'42   77–26300
ISBN 0–582–48935–0

Printed in Great Britain at The Spottiswoode Ballantyne Press, by William Clowes & Sons Limited, London, Colchester and Beccles

Contents

Editors' Preface

In this book, Kenneth Roberts has written a successor to the title originally contributed to the Series by our late friend and colleague, Professor Gordon Rose of Manchester University. We feel he would have liked it.

The Social Structure of Modern Britain Series has been designed to meet the needs of students following a variety of academic and professional courses in universities, polytechnics, colleges of higher education, colleges of education, and colleges of further education. Although principally of interest to social scientists, the Series does not attempt a comprehensive treatment of the whole field of sociology, but concentrates on the social structure of modern Britain which forms a central feature of most such tertiary-level courses in this country. Its purpose is to offer an analysis of our contemporary society through the study of basic demographic, ideological and structural features, and the examination of such major social institutions as the family, education, the economic and political structure, and religion. The aim has been to produce a series of introductory texts which will in combination form the basis for a sustained course of study, but each volume has been designed as a single whole and can be read in its own right.

We hope that the topics covered in the series will prove attractive to a wide reading public and that, in addition to students, others who wish to know more than is readily available about the nature and structure of their own society will find them of interest.

JOHN BARRON MAYS
MAURICE CRAFT

Foreword

There is more than a grain of substance in the jocular definition of sociology as the study of social class. Stratification has always been a major area of sociological enquiry, and rightly so, for it is so useful a theme through which to explore the inter-connections between the various parts of a social system. Hence the difficulty in locating studies of any aspect of life in contemporary Britain in which the working class does not make an appearance. By all definitions, the working class encompasses the bulk of the population, and therefore a systematic examination of the British working class necessarily develops into an analysis of British society in general. This book surveys the now considerable literature on the working class. It offers a digest of relevant research and a guide to the major theoretical controversies. Sociologists, I hope, will find its arguments interesting. Students of contemporary Britain should also find the book useful.

As author and following convention, I accept sole responsibility for errors and omissions, but I would like to acknowledge assistance received from various quarters in writing this volume. Firstly, I thank the Editors of this series for their helpful suggestions, and for the opportunity they originally offered to produce a successor to the late Professor Gordon Rose's earlier volume. Secondly, I am indebted to my colleague Stan Clark for his vigorous but constructive criticism. Finally, but certainly not least, my thanks are due to Margaret Grek for her speedy and accurate typing of the manuscript.

The debate about the working class

Industrialism and class analysis

The industrial revolution inspired a new kind of class analysis. All societies have been stratified, meaning that valued resources such as income, wealth and power have been distributed unequally. Social equality has been a long-applauded ideal but never fully practised. Functionalists say stratification is universal because it alone can perform essential functions in whose absence no society could endure, and that condemning inequality is misguided. In opposition, conflict theorists argue that whilst some inequalities may be necessary to motivate and reward individuals in accordance with their contributions to society, actual inequalities mostly reflect the success of advantaged groups in securing privileges.

Whilst some type of stratification has been a universal fact of life, inequalities have not followed the same pattern in all societies, and in nineteenth-century Europe amidst the industrial revolution and its related socio-political transformations, social thinkers became aware that new forms of inequality were taking shape. Medieval European societies had been seen as divided into orders or estates – the aristocracy, peasantry, burghers and church, each with a prescribed role and surrounded by its own legally defined rights and duties. Members of different estates were subject to different laws, differed in their political representation and were liable to the justice of different courts. Other forms of inequality had prevailed elsewhere. Slavery had been widely practised. Slaves enjoy negligible or no social rights and are treated as the chattels of free-men whose right to use their 'property' as they choose may be unlimited. India was traditionally stratified into castes; groups considered blessed with different degrees of religious purity and risking pollution through contact with the impure. Each caste had a prescribed way of life which stipulated, for example, the types of work that individuals were to undertake. Castes were entered by birth, and mobility during a person's lifetime was all but impossible.

The systems of inequality that became prominent in nineteenth-century Europe alongside the rise of industrialism clearly differed from these known forms of stratification, and the term 'class' entered general use to describe the emergent strata. It was not a new expression, but along with other concepts including industry, secularization and community that were being redefined to make the emergent society intelligible, 'class' acquired a new meaning. Its use helped distinguish the new from traditional forms of inequality. Firstly, classes differed from estates and castes in their openness. There were no legal or religious barriers preventing individuals improving their class positions. In the jargon of modern sociology, class positions are achieved rather than ascribed. Secondly, members of all classes enjoyed the same legal status. They were judged by exactly the same laws and courts. Class divisions were decreed by neither law nor religion. Economic position was the basic arbiter. An individual's standing in the class structure depended upon the type of occupation he practised and his success within it. If people were successful and made money whether from manufacturing, trade or commerce, then irrespective of their social origins, religion and politics this was sufficient to elevate their class positions.

In the nineteenth century the contours of the emergent class structure were clearly visible to neither the founding fathers of sociology nor the rest of the public. Issues such as whether the *nouveau riche* deserved the respect previously reserved for landed gentry haunted respectable drawing rooms and novels of the period, whilst the desirability of opening the universities and civil service to non-Anglicans were controversial issues. Meanwhile sociologists engaged in parallel debates to render their changing society comprehensible. There were various attempts to make sense of the new class structure, all controversial, but none more influential than the contribution of Karl Marx. He remains the only sociologist whose name has become an *ism* and whose theories have inspired a worldwide social movement.

Since his own lifetime, Marx has been *the* figure that other social theorists have been unable to ignore. Even dissenters have been obliged at least to offer reasoned replies.

Marx defined social classes as aggregates of individuals standing in common relationships to the means of production and, in the capitalist society that was maturing in his lifetime, he identified two principal classes; the capitalists or bougeoisie who owned the means of production, and the workers or proletariat who sold their labour for wages. In actual fact Marx never over-simplified as crudely as the above statement implies. He distinguished a variety of class situations, realizing, for example, that the interests of landed strata could differ from the owners of industrial capital, and that the petit bourgeoisie of small-shopkeepers along with self-employed artisans and professional people occupied an ambiguous position between the major classes. Nevertheless, he envisaged that over time capitalist society would become polarized into its two principal classes with intermediate strata being forced into one or the other. Marx distinguished between a 'class in itself' and a 'class for itself'. He realized that the members of a class might fail to recognize their common position and interests. Given time and experience of its exploited condition, however, Marx believed that the proletariat would become a class-conscious revolutionary force. He regarded the interests of bourgeoisie and proletariat as inherently antagonistic. The capitalists' interest was profit which required denying the worker the full value of his labour. Marx envisaged a time when workers would realize that overthrowing the social relations of capitalism would enable them to enjoy the full fruits of the forces of production. Earlier historical epochs, in Marx's view, had contained comparable antagonistic class relationships out of which more advanced social orders had evolved, and in time he believed that a further epoch of socialism would be born.

A quasi-Marxist working class

In Britain Marx's revolutionary predictions still await fulfilment. Capitalism has not only survived the century since Marx's death; political parties claiming Marxist inspiration have never even enjoyed mass support. Much that Marx wrote has proved wrong, but he shares this distinction with all his contemporaries. Within sociology Marx has no 'fundamentalist' disciples who insist upon defending every phrase and comma in the 'holy scriptures'. Present-day Marxist sociologists do not claim that Marx supplied all the answers, but that his questions and general approach to the analysis of social systems – his methodology – remains the most fruitful. Within capitalist societies there may be relations to the means of production other than owners and workers. It can be argued, for example, that managers who exercise authority or the middle classes who sell expertise and motivation in addition to brute labour power are distinguishable classes with special interests, and that patterns of conflict other than between bourgeoisie and proletariat are important sources of historical change. Many western Marxists now reject the view that the supercession of capitalism necessarily results in a classless society. One school of thought identifies the cadres who man state apparatuses and therefore control the means of production in socialist countries as a new dominant class.

Once we resist assessing Marx by fortune-telling standards we can see that many subsequent trends have been consistent with his basic perspectives. To begin with, although the proletariat has not inspired a revolution, the majority of blue-collar workers identify themselves as working class, are organized in trade unions and support the Labour Party. Calling oneself working class does not necessarily imply class consciousness in the Marxist sense, but it indicates that individuals are at least class aware; that they acknowledge the existence of divisions cutting right across society, and recognize some interests shared by workers in different industries, firms and occupations. Likewise trade union membership and Labour Party voting are scarcely revolutionary activities, but they indicate a willingness to participate in collective action, a recognition that workers must organize to protect their interests, and some vision, however vague, of a better society. This evidence can be construed as indicating that at least a section of the proletariat is partway towards developing the revolutionary conscious- ness that Marx predicted. Other interpretations of the evidence are certainly possible, but this Marxist account is by no means ludicrous. Westergaard and Resler[1] show how plausible it can sound.

They argue that the pattern of inequality in modern Britain continues to reflect the class interests that Marx originally identified. 'Property, profit and market – the key institutions of capitalist society – retain their central place in social arrangements, and remain the prime determinants of inequality.'[2] Furthermore, 'The range and shape of income inequality in Britain reflects the fact that the economy is still, in all essentials, capitalist'.[3]

Whilst a concerted challenge to capitalism is still awaited, Westergaard and Resler attach some significance to manual workers' recognition that they belong to a working class, and to their long-standing commitment to a broad labour movement in industry and politics that has consistently developed visions of a better and fairer society. These authors argue that the radicalization of the entire proletariat remains a distinct possibility and are alert to signs of its imminence including the growth of shop-floor militancy since the 1950s and, since the 1960s, the escalation of wage expectations that capitalism cannot satisfy. An explosion of working class consciousness and revolutionary action may be less likely than this analysis suggests, but it is difficult to quarrel with Westergaard and Resler's verdict that the manual working class is 'quasi-Marxist' in character.

Sociologists are interested in subjective aspects of stratification including the classes with which individuals align themselves because individuals' beliefs are part of the reality of social class. Jarvie has drawn an analogy between social class and money.[4] The latter works only if people believe in it. If the public loses confidence in a currency it ceases to perform the functions associated with money. Likewise the effects of inequalities depend upon how individuals perceive, appraise and react to them. Jarvie ridicules the 'castle and gate' view which presumes that classes exist ready-made awaiting discovery by members of the public; '. . . just because our language contains the words "social class" we are not free to assume that there is some clear and definite concept here which corresponds to a part of the world and towards definition of which we should strive.'[5] Jarvie's argument is that classes are not encountered ready-made but are constructed from ordinary people's beliefs. 'My position is that what sustains the reality of the system of social class is that real people believe in it and act on these beliefs. . . .

My view, that people have *theories* of class, and that they act *as if* these theories were true, adequately explains the "class" phenomena.'[6] Jarvie does not imagine that laymen acquire beliefs in a fortuitous manner. The material inequalities that individuals encounter in the distribution of income, wealth, education, housing and other resources help to inspire and endorse popular beliefs. But once an interpretation of these inequalities becomes prevalent, this adds to and qualitatively changes the class situation. When individuals coordinate their beliefs into an inter-subjective consensus, the referents acquire an objective quality. This happens with money: pieces of paper behave like money whilst everyone believes in their ability to purchase goods and services. Similarly if the majority of manual workers share a belief that they constitute a working class, this class becomes a phenomenon with which employers and politicians have to contend.

Hence it is of some significance that the majority of Britain's manual workers *do* identify themselves as working class. Surveys conducted throughout the last thirty years have consistently shown that this is how they mostly describe themselves in response to open-ended questions.[7] Table 1.1 presents the results from a National Opinion Poll in which respondents were invited to identify with a social class. In the table, groups A, B and C1 cover white-collar jobs, whilst C2, D and E represent skilled, semi-skilled and unskilled manual occupations. People's answers depend upon how the questions are phrased; whether an initial 'Don't know' is followed by further probing, and whether the investigators allow respondents to employ unusual terms in describing themselves. But all enquiries, whatever their methodological peculiarities, have found that the majority of manual workers align themselves with a working class.

Table 1.1 Occupations and subjective social class (in percentages)

Subjective social class	Occupational group			
	AB	C1	C2	DE
Middle	82	73	43	35
Working	13	24	53	59
Don't knows	5	3	4	6

Source. From National Opinion Polls, Bulletin 109, 1972.

Needless to say, there are plenty of 'deviants' who identify with different classes. Over a third of manual workers regard themselves as middle class. Others employ less common labels such as lower, respectable and labouring. But whereas most white-collar employees describe themselves as middle class, amongst manual workers these identifiers are a minority. Individuals in all types and grades of manual work mostly see themselves as working class. The situation is admittedly more complicated than even this qualified statement suggests. Working-class identifiers do not possess totally identical beliefs about the class structure. The working class label can be prefixed with lower, upper, skilled and a variety of other terms. There are bewildering variations in the public's everyday conceptions of class. Indeed, the same individual's views can change over a short period of time. In a study which involved detailed questioning to probe people's conceptions of the class structure, Hiller found 10 per cent of his respondents changing their views on the number of classes that existed, often without being aware of their inconsistency, during the course of a single interview.[8] Moorhouse also found respondents contradicting themselves when he re-interviewed a mainly blue-collar sample some months after the initial enquiry.[9] Sociologists would obviously be unwise to attach much significance to beliefs that are so fickle. Working-class identifiers vary considerably in their attitudes towards members of other classes. Some manual workers admire and wish to emulate their betters, seek promotion and encourage their children to 'get on', whilst others speak of more privileged classes as the 'other side'. Some working-class identifiers demand a redistribution of privilege in favour of their own class, whilst others are complacent or resigned to their deprivations.[10]

Beneath the variations, however, there are recurrent themes.[11] There is a modal working class image of society in which this class is defined as the largest bottom group, which regards many existing inequalities as unjust, and which favours social change to rectify these inequalities. This image of society incorporates solidaristic sentiments. Members of the working class sympathize with the misfortunes of their peers and support their struggles. An appreciation of a need to stand together in mutual support is found both in neighbourhood communities and in broader working class organizations including trade unions and the Labour Party. The deviations from this type of imagery are numerous and significant, but the existence of a modal form of working class awareness is at least equally important.

Another complication is that class awareness can vary in salience. People might describe themselves as working class when interviewed by sociologists, but it will not *necessarily* follow that this awareness will colour their attitudes and behaviour in everyday situations. Individuals have statuses and interests other than those associated with their class identities. The same people who are working class are also husbands, fathers, gardeners, soccer fans and consumers. However, whilst recognizing that individuals have alternative frames of reference, the manual strata's working class awareness cannot be dismissed as trivial. It is simply untrue to suggest that workers only think about social class when so invited by sociologists. All the evidence indicates that class is especially salient amongst manual workers. When asked to explain their political loyalties and to describe 'people like themselves', manual employees who identify with the working class are more likely to reply in 'class' terms than any other section of the public.[12]

Manual work is associated not only with working class identification, but also with trade union membership. Once again there are numerous exceptions to the rule. In 1974, 42 per cent of all manual workers, who tend to be scattered in the smaller establishments where it is difficult for unions to recruit and provide a service, were *not* trade unionists. Amongst those who are members, the majority are in no sense activists. Many join only because the 'closed shop' makes it a condition of employment and remain suspicious of trade union power.[13] Nevertheless, the fact that trade unionism has advanced to the position where it can virtually enforce membership throughout much of large-scale industry testifies to a persistent grass-roots appeal. White-collar trade unionists are far from uncommon. In 1974, 39 per cent of all white-collar workers were unionized and comprised the most rapidly growing section of the entire trade union movement.[14] As the data in Table 1.2 show, trade union membership throughout the entire labour force has been growing since the mid 1960s and the rate of increase has been particularly rapid amongst white-collar workers. The significance of these trends is currently a matter for debate. According to one view, the growing density of white-collar unionism indicates that a range of formerly middle class occupations are being proletarianized. Another argument alleges that trade unionism is ceasing to be a class movement; that rather than representing 'labour' in general, the unions are increasingly articulating the sectional and sometimes conflicting interests of a host of particular occupational groups. Notwithstanding the trends inspiring these theories, however, trade unionism remains significantly stronger amongst manual employees, implying the more widespread recognition that workers share interests in common, that the employment relationship involves bargaining conflicting interests, and that securing improvements in pay and other conditions of work depends upon collective action.

Table 1.2   Density of trade union membership

Percentages of workers in trade unions	1948	1964	1974
(a) White-collar	30·2	29·6	39·4
(b) Manual	50·7	52·9	57·9

Source.   Figures from R. Price and G S Bain, 'Union growth revisited: 1948-1974 in perspective', *British Journal of Industrial Relations* 14 (1976) 339–55.

A third characteristic of manual workers is that the majority who vote support the Labour Party (see Table 1.3). Once again there are thousands of blue-collar 'deviants' who vote Conservative or Liberal, just as a minority of white-collar employees vote Labour. Deviant voters are as welcome as any others to their favoured parties, but the Labour Party cannot ignore the fact that over three-quarters of its votes are from manual households. In terms of voter characteristics, Labour is Britain's working class party. It is the most popular choice amongst all grades of manual workers. The Conservative Party, in contrast, knows that its appeal is thinly spread in working class areas whilst it can rely on dense support in predominantly middle class suburbs. Labour voting need not imply that manual workers are committed socialists. In most cases their commitment to the Labour Party does not extend beyond voting at general elections, and surveys repeatedly show that many of Labour's blue-collar voters are critical of further nationalization and tolerant of capitalism.[15] But as the findings of the National Opinion Polls in Table 1.4 illustrate, manual workers are distinctly less likely to be suspicious of trade union power and more likely to be critical of profit than white-collar employees. The mass blue-collar vote that the Labour Party has consistently won since the Second World War suggests a reservoir of working class support for a political programme designed to redistribute privilege and, when necessary, to attack the interests and curb the power of currently dominant strata.

Table 1.3   Voting intentions in October 1974 (in percentages)

| | Occupational group | | | | | |
	A	B	C1	C2	D	E
Conservative	68	60	46	30	25	34
Labour	14	20	28	50	59	52

Source. Gallup Polls, 1974.

Table 1.4   Attitudes of occupational strata

	AB	C1	C2	DE
Percentages saying that companies make too much profit*	9	27	38	39
Percentages saying that trade unions have too much power†	76	75	61	53

*National Opinion Polls, 1970.

†National Opinion Polls, 1969.

Working class identification, trade union membership and Labour voting are not only all similarly associated with manual employment. They are also related to each other. Manual workers who describe themselves as working class tend to be the same individuals who are organized in trade unions and who support the Labour Party. Working class identifiers often explain their political loyalties in terms of Labour being 'the party for the working man'. Conversely, the deviants who align themselves with the middle class tend to be the same individuals who also deviate from their class norm by voting Conservative and remaining outside the trade union movement.[16] Hence we have a syndrome of inter-related characteristics that separate the manual segment from the remainder of the population. There appears to be something about a particular type of employment, manual work, that encourages people to regard themselves as working class, whilst a perception of belonging to this working class mobilizes support for trade unions and the Labour Party. The net result is a cleavage in society that divides the population according to their types of work, the sides of the table they align with in industrial relations and their political partisanship. This cleavage is not a figment of the sociological imagination. Sociology has not invented the working class. Sociology merely records, then seeks to clarify and explain the implications of this schism in the social structure. The implications are manifold for, as we shall see, whatever other aspects of social behaviour are examined, differences between the working class and the rest repeatedly appear.

By now it will be apparent why this chapter did not open with a concise definition of the working class. When analysing survey data it is sometimes convenient to use one factor, usually occupation, as an index of individuals' class positions, but the working class is not *just* the aggregate of manual workers, nor *just* people who happen to regard themselves as working class. The concept draws attention to how these and other factors interrelate to form a class phenomenon that is something more than the mere sum of its elements. If this exposition sounds vague it is only to remain true to reality. The above discussion should have destroyed any hopes that the boundaries of the working class might be precisely charted. If all manual workers described themselves as working class and voted Labour it would aid sociological analysis, but there are numerous exceptions. It would also be convenient for sociology if working and middle class attitudes were diametrically opposed on every conceivable issue, but in practice there is considerable overlapping. As seen in Table 1.4, the middle classes are the more suspicious of trade union power and the less critical of profit, but there are many working class identifiers in blue-collar jobs who agree with the middle classes on these points. The break between the middle and working classes is not crystal clear, though the blurred boundary in no way detracts from the reality of this schism.

It is not straightforward even to say exactly which occupations are manual. There are categorizing schemes in general use, including that employed by the Registrar-General to analyse census data, which appear to place every occupation unambiguously in either a manual or non-manual category, but the basis of these classifications is only commonsense rule-of-thumb. With most occupations commonsense leaves little doubt, but there are dozens of jobs including the various types of shopwork, supervisory posts and technical occupations where commonsense is fuzzy. We will see in the next chapter that, like the working class concept, manual work can be adequately defined only in terms of a set of interrelated characteristics and this inevitably means that some occupations will fall neither unambiguously inside nor outside the category.

Both Rallings[17] and Jary[18] have noted that since the 1950s the proportion of white-collar votes won by the Labour Party has increased. Formerly blue-collar 'defectors' out-numbered white-collar 'deviants'; the middle classes voted more solidly Conservative then the working class voted Labour. At the time of the 1974 general elections, however, just over a third of each group supported the 'other side's' party, and within the white-collar strata Labour support was especially prevalent amongst the younger voters. A substantial block of this new Labour support is from individuals in the least prestigious non-manual jobs whose behaviour and attitudes manifest more general 'proletarian' traits. For instance, density of trade union membership is as high as amongst the manual strata and working class identification is common.[19] There is evidence that these developments reflect a proletarianization of what have formerly been considered white-collar jobs, meaning that in terms of pay and promotion prospects, for example, the occupations have become less distinguishable from manual work. If this trend has been occurring it implies that the ceiling of the 'manual' category and also the working class is being revised upwards. The details need not concern us here, but the issue illustrates that the boundary between manual and other occupations is fluid rather than precisely fixed for all time.

Comparative perspectives

Sometimes Britain is named as a particularly class-ridden society, but none of the actual evidence indicates that her class differences are especially severe. The rate of social mobility is similar in other western countries.[20] In all western societies the terms middle and working class or equivalents are in general use, trade union membership is especially dense and militant amongst manual workers[21] and this cleavage is reflected in party political alignments.

The *appearance* of rigidity in Britain's class structure could be due to a number of circumstances. To begin with, other sources of conflict are less evident than elsewhere leaving class divisions highly exposed. Britain is so overwhelmingly urbanized that a town–country division cannot become politically prominent. In addition, Britain has possessed a sufficiently uniform national culture to inhibit the growth of regionally-based political parties, though the recent rise of nationalist movements in Scotland and (to a lesser extent) Wales is changing this scene. Ethnic minorities are too small to rival social classes as foundations for political movements, whilst religious differences, outside Northern Ireland, have hardly intruded into political life. In the outside world religion is a more common source of political loyalties than Britons tend to realize. Rose and Urwin's research into the 76 major political parties in 17 western countries found that 35 had a religious base whilst 33, in 14 countries, based their ideologies and support on social classes.[22] This proves that class-based politics is not peculiarly British. At the same time, it shows that in many countries class is only one amongst other bases of political division. Another explanation of her apparently harsh class divisions concerns the evolutionary character of the social changes that accompanied industrialization in Britain. Former dominant groups were not toppled and stripped of their wealth and power but assimilated with the rising bourgeoisie, shrouding the middle classes with an aristocratic aura and emphasising the cultural chasm above the working class. An additional point concerns Britain's status as the first industrial nation. Britain's labour movement now rests on over a century's history. It is sometimes argued that values which have become entrenched in the Labour Party and trade unions were forged under conditions prevailing generations ago which have now changed, rendering the values inappropriate. In reply, it is just as plausible to argue that other industrial countries will eventually face equally well-developed forms of working class awareness and organization.

A working class can be discerned in other western countries, but whether the same is true of the socialist world is less certain. One school of thought emphasises the differences between stratification in socialist and capitalist societies. Goldthorpe[23] argues that when the flow of resources is subject to central political regulation, a different pattern of inequality should be expected than where market forces are allowed greater reign, and Hollander[24] offers numerous illustrations of how inequalities in the Soviet Union discord with western experience. In the USSR there are elites of relatively highly-paid and prestigious workers in virtually all occupations; manual workers are not threatened by unemployment whilst high-ranking bureaucrats are liable to dismissal with no prospect of alternative careers; goods including housing which are marketed in western countries are distributed as social services. A number of writers have suggested that the different principles governing inequality prevent a schism between the manual and non-manual strata appearing in socialist societies. Giddens,[25] Parkin[26] and Wesolowski[27] all claim an overlapping of occupational prestige, earnings, educational levels, job security and access to bonus payments across manual and the more routine white-collar occupations. Other analysts, however, read the evidence differently. Lane comments on the wide income disparities that persist in the USSR.[28] Government ministers earn nine times the average income, whilst plant directors typically receive thirteen times their lowest grade workers' earnings.

Lane also argues that when all fringe benefits and housing allocations are taken into account, a definite division between the white- and blue-collar strata *does* become evident in the Soviet Union.[29] Some writers allege that inequalities under socialist regimes do not give rise to *antagonistic* class divisions since rewards can depend not upon possession or non-possession of property but purely upon individuals' contributions to their society.[30] Other commentators, however, identify grounds for potential conflict between workers and the bureaucrats who tend to monopolise power and amass privileges.

The existence of a working class expressing its interests through its own political and industrial organizations is not a peculiarly British phenomenon. Though sometimes less prominent, a parallel cleavage is found in all western countries, but whether comparable patterns of inequality, class awareness and action are generated under socialism is a question for further evidence and discussion. Whilst the following chapters deal specifically with the British working class, the arguments have a wider relevance, but *exactly* how wide is one of the issues surrounding the working class currently open for debate.

The issues

Our aim is to press beyond these preliminary comments to a more comprehensive exploration of the cleavage that separates the working class, to discuss the significance of this division for society at large and to consider its implications for the likely direction of social change. On these issues the diagnosis that still challenges everyone else is the Marxist position, already briefly described. Capitalist societies are seen as divided by the conflicting interests of owners and non-owners of the means of production. Whilst the entire proletariat has not become class conscious, Marxist writers argue that manual workers' circumstances have provoked an at least partial awareness of their exploited position. Marxists talk the language of class struggle, portray the working class as exploited and alienated by the logic of capitalism, yet simultaneously generating resistance and glimpses of a socialist future.

In sociology Marxism's main rival has been the functionalist theory which regards inequality as an inevitable fact of life performing necessary functions for society as a whole. Just as there are different Marxisms, there are several functionalist explanations of inequality but they possess common features. Firstly they stress a need for a minimal consensus on values and norms if any social system is to endure; that total dissensus would mean anarchy rather than a society. Secondly they stress a need for individuals to be rewarded depending upon how their social positions and performances earn approval from whatever values are operative. Inequalities are seen as incentives, motivating people to behave as the social system requires. Thirdly, functionalists stress how inequalities publicly applaud virtue thereby reinforcing the values that allow society to cohere. According to this theory, stratification generates not conflict but social integration. Fusing these propositions leads to a functionalist model of a stratified society. The social hierarchy is conceived not as composed of discrete classes but as a continuous scale with positions ranked and rewarded according to their merits as indicated by the common value system. The model treats individuals at all levels as acknowledging the rightfulness of prevailing inequalities which embody values to which the entire population subscribes. Privilege is regarded as stimulating approbation rather than antagonism, and as motivating individuals to conform with society's values rather than to attack the reward structure.

Functionalists acknowledge that no actual system of stratification conforms wholly with their model. Whilst arguing that some system of stratification is inevitable and functional for every society, they recognize that inequalities can become dysfunctional as when powerful groups use their influence to amass privileges purely in their own interests. They also acknowledge that denying rewards to individuals in low status positions can be a disincentive to effort, and that the less privileged are liable to nurture deviant values resulting in a sense of injustice and social conflict. Bernard Barber attaches all these qualifications in his examination of stratification in America, but nevertheless stresses how inequalities integrate the community by expressing common values and perform an 'adaptive' function by motivating individuals to act in ways that their society approves.[31] Although he admits blemishes, Barber argues that inequalities are distributed along a continuous scale, and that dividing the population into classes is more a matter of descriptive convenience than a true portrait of reality. Dennis Wrong, another American sociologist, argues that the trends in his society are towards ironing out breaks in the social hierarchy, leaving individuals scattered at different points along a sliding scale of inequality, and terms this condition 'inequality without stratification'.[32] According to this view, the American class structure bears a sufficiently close resemblance to the functionalist model for the latter to remain the most useful theoretical perspective. Needless to say, Marxists are in complete disagreement.

Functionalist and conflict theorists who draw their principal inspiration from Marx continue to engage in heated debate. To many sociologists, however, these 'grand theories' seem ill-equipped to cope with the complexities of contemporary life. Just as Marx claims few if any fundamentalist disciples, so functionalism has few outright defenders. Treating an examination of the British working class as an opportunity to debate the respective merits of functionalism and Marxism, therefore, may not be the most fruitful approach. Fortunately we need not abandon theory in favour of a pretence of letting the facts speak for themselves. Since the 1950s a concern to bring sociological theory into closer contact with reality has seen the grand theories spawning more specific ideas, including some about the present-day working class, and the validity of these ideas does not have to rest upon their more ambitious parents' claims to universal truth.

Functionalism's claim to supply a universal explanation of stratification can be placed to one side, leaving a set of sympathetic arguments which regard the position of the working class as changing to increasingly resemble the functionalist model. Whereas in the past a relatively clear break encouraged manual workers to regard themselves as a working class and to conceive their interests as conflicting with other groups, it is argued that as modern societies recover from the trauma of industrialization the trend is towards healing the rift. Attention is drawn to post-Keynesian economic management, the maintenance of full employment and greater security for manual workers. The argument emphasizes the growth of the welfare state, and how it has transformed previously middle class privileges into universal rights. Altogether a diverse set of trends are blended into the analysis. We are told about the demise of authoritarian management in the face of trade union power, and employment legislation that has restricted bosses' rights to hire and fire. Then there is technological progress which, it is argued, is continuously taking the labour out of manual work and increasing the demand for technical skills and training. In the large modern corporation, it is claimed that not only salaried staff but manual workers as well can be treated as *members* of firms which offer stability of earnings, secure jobs and a range of fringe benefits. In industry the traditional distinction between staff and works is seen as breaking down, whilst outside the workplace affluent manual workers emulate middle class life-styles. In housing and access to a range of consumer goods the life-styles of the former middle and working classes are seen as merging. Aggregating all these trends, the majority of all workers by hand and brain are portrayed as fusing into a middle mass. The phrase 'working class' may remain in the vocabulary, but rather then referring to a *real* group aware of possessing distinctive interests that conflict with other classes', the working class is seen as becoming a purely nominal label which enables both researchers and ordinary members of the public to distinguish the lower rungs in the social hierarchy. This interpretation of on-going currents of change will be examined in Chapters 2 and 3.

In addition to functionalism and Marxism there is a third branch of grand theory, originally inspired by Max Weber. Orthodox Marxism regards other inequalities, in the final analysis, as reflecting the antagonistic interests of classes standing in different relationships to the means of production. Weber dissented and distinguished class, status and power as separable dimensions of stratification which interacted but nevertheless remained irreducible to one another. Hence the Weberian, multi-dimensional view of stratification.[33] This perspective opens research into topics that the functionalist and Marxist approaches are unlikely to suggest. It has led, for example, to studies of status consistency, congruence or crystallization. Members of a population can be placed in separate rank orders in terms of income, wealth, education, housing, occupational prestige and a host of other variables. When this is accomplished a positive correlation between individuals' positions in the differnt hierarchies is invariably discovered, but cases of incongruence or inconsistency do arise, and there is now a body of literature exploring the consequences. How do individuals cope with ambiguities in their social positions? This question need not delay us here for, as regards the working class, the issue that the multi-dimensional theory raises concerns the pervasiveness of this rift in the social structure. One school of thought accepts that the division of labour in industry involves a schism between the working class and super-ordinate strata but queries the extent to which this cleavage is reflected in non-working life. Weber's concept of status refers to a dimension of stratification where life-styles are ranked according to their degrees of honour. It was Weber's view that the contours of this status hierarchy could differ from class divisions rooted in the system of economic production, and that class and status, therefore, comprised alternative bases from which sections of a population could develop an awareness of mutual interests and organize politically. Chapters 4 and 5, which deal with variations in family and community life, and educational opportunity, appraise the relevance of the working class concept as we move away from the workplace and interests that arise directly therein.

Marxism intrudes throughout the discussion. Inevitably so, since the alternative grand theories arose largely as challenges. Marx believed that capitalist societies contained in-built tendencies towards polariz-ation with class divisions becoming increasingly clear and members conscious of their conflicting interests. By viewing the structure of inequality differently, the functionalist and Weberian perspectives, if adopted, make us less likely to anticipate such developments. Marxist sociologists, in contrast, have continued to insist upon the revolution-ary *potential* of the working class and have addressed their thoughts to why the revolution has not yet happened. Why does the working class allow itself to remain imprisoned in capitalist relationships? One answer suggests that, to date, the working class has failed to gain the upper hand in the class struggle. It is alleged that bourgeois values are imposed upon the working class in work situations, through political institutions, education, religion and the mass media. As a result, working class opposition is contained, the escalation of revolutionary consciousness is inhibited and the prolet-ariat is incorporated as an unstable force within capitalist society.

Others argue that the working class is acting as a source of social change but neither in the ways nor with the effect that Marx originally predicted. It is said that change is occurring gradually as working class interests are articulated through the Labour Party and trade unions. Through evolution rather than revolution the net result is presented as a transformation of capitalism. This argument leads to descriptions of present day society as socially pluralist, as a liberal democracy, or as a post-capitalist welfare state. According to this view, capitalist institutions survive but have lost their former dominance. Another explanation of the revolution's failure to erupt claims that manual workers' circumstances do *not* generate the kind of radical conscious-ness that Marx envisaged. It is argued that whilst some manual workers' milieux are conducive to a form of proletarian awareness, other sections of the working class are more likely to develop deferential or money-model images of society. These alternative accounts of the position of the working class in the power structure, which are discussed in Chapter 6, cannot all be described as Marxist, but it is the Marxist perspective that identifies the problem being addressed as critical.

No one could portray the working class as under-researched. It features in every conceivable area of social enquiry. 'The working class' is one of the most frequently-used terms in sociology's vocabulary. There are studies of education and the working class, religion and the working class, politics and the working class. Indeed, across every area of investigation sociologists have probed the peculiarities of working class attitudes and behaviour. Discussing the working class does not require speculation on the basis of sparse evidence. The sheer weight of data is immense and most of it has been collected only recently. Whilst sociology's origins can be traced beyond the nineteenth century, in Britain its take-off and growth into a staple academic discipline has occurred only since the 1950s and the bulk of research on the working class has been undertaken subsequently. This research has yielded a plethora of data, and rather than a shortage of evidence, sociology's current problem is to decide what the evidence means; to prevent the issues being buried by the data their investigation has produced. The questions outlined above offer a route through the evidence whilst keeping sight of the larger theoretical controversies surrounding the working class. These questions are best regarded as complementary. Rather than leading to alternative answers each claiming to offer *the* correct interpretation of the contemporary working class, the questions raise different issues. Is the traditional division between the working and middle class being closed? In so far as this schism persists, what is its breadth and depth? On any account the working class is an under-class, so why does not the social system collapse under the burden of working class dissent?

The following chapters will survey these issues along with the evidence that can be quoted in support of the various answers, but since the working class is a controversial subject there is inevitably an author's argument. No one with the interest to write about the working class could claim to be a neutral guide through the literature. Summarily stated, I argue that the working class is a valid but often over-worked concept; valid in tapping a continuing cleavage in the social structure which is not being closed by occupational, economic and related currents of change. The following chapters invite scepticism towards functionalist-inspired theories claiming that the rift above the working class is being healed. At the same time, the presentation warns against imagining that working and middle class values are opposed on every conceivable issue and that all types of inequality fall neatly away from the working–middle class divide. The argument is sympathetic to the Weberian vision of inequality as multi-dimensional. This is one reason why the working class has not polarized in total opposition to the social order, but it will be argued that there are many additional reasons including the fact that a convincing and simultaneously appealing agenda for change has yet to be offered. Whilst oppositional, it is therefore argued that the working class is unlikely to develop into the revolutionary force that orthodox Marxists have envisaged. Overworking the working class concept means exaggerating its radical impetus, deprivations and discontents. This volume warns against trying to make the working class explain so much that reality is obscured instead of clarified. Suitably forewarned, readers may wish to draw contrary conclusions from the evidence and arguments presented.

Work

'Aren't we all working class?', asks the managing director. 'Don't we all work for our livings?' Every investigator who solicits the public's views on social class is guaranteed a deluge of such remarks. The speakers rarely take themselves so seriously as to actually describe themselves as working class, but the majority of middle class identifiers refuse to regard their own class as a privileged stratum above a larger working class. This working class image of society is not reciprocated by 'them'. And this should occasion little surprise, for however society appears from the factory floor the majority of white-collar workers can hardly be expected to regard themselves as part of an undifferentiated, well-rewarded élite. One middle class image conceives society as a prestige hierarchy containing numerous rungs but with no dramatic break at any point. Another defines the middle class as the largest class occupying the central ground in the social structure and encompassing the majority of both blue- and white-collar employees.[1] To white-collar workers who see society in these terms, it appears odd when manual workers insist on setting themselves apart and claim to belong to a separate *working* class. What is it about manual work that encourages this type of imagery?

Manual workers are not always the lower paid. There is considerable overlapping between blue- and white-collar pay levels. One view, to be discussed in the next chapter, contends that this overlapping is becoming increasingly extensive and that today's salary levels often lag behind. For the meantime suffice it to note that many manual workers cannot conceivably be described as low paid. Oil-rig workers together with many craftsmen in building trades and shipyards can boast pay packets to excite envy in school staff rooms. The poor and the working class are not interchangeable expressions. Has anyone not heard of the affluent manual worker? There are school caretakers and railway employees whose earnings would not tempt any managers from their offices. Some manual jobs are low paid, but remain so largely because better-paid groups insist upon maintaining their differentials. Meanwhile some non-manual workers, including police constables, can claim to be in low-paid occupations.

Standards of living depend not only upon individuals' earnings. Low pay need not entail poverty. Domestic circumstances make a difference. Today over a half of all married women are in paid employment, and working class affluence is based largely upon their contributions to household budgets. In families containing a single wage-earner and dependent children, an above-average income will not guarantee an affluent life-style. In contrast, when two wage-earners are supporting no dependents, their individual incomes need not be above average to permit holidays, trips to clubs and visits to the cinema. These are amongst the facts of life that managers and their kind ponder when suggesting that, in any meaningful sense, virtually everyone must be considered working class.

Yet in point of fact manual work is different. At least it has been to the present. Blue-collar jobs differ in numerous ways that are only too evident to the incumbents. There is a school of thought, most popular amongst American commentators, contending that manual occupations are gradually losing their special working class character, and this argument will be considered shortly. To begin with, however, let us examine the 'traditional' features of their jobs that have encouraged manual workers to regard themselves as working class.

Career patterns

Blue-collar wage levels are not consistently inferior to white-collar salaries but they move in a different way during the course of working life. Male white-collar employees normally benefit from incremental salary scales and progressive careers. The young police constable may earn less than many factory workers but he is unlikely to remain a constable throughout his working life. Similarly beginning teachers, local government officers and bank clerks can bemoan their less than average earnings, but have colleagues in their fifties who can voice no equivalent complaints. White-collar salary levels improve progressively with age and peak only in the period immediately preceding retirement. Furthermore, it is not only the salary that grows as a non-manual career develops. Salaried staff acquire seniority, status and authority. A blue-collar working life rarely offers these experiences.

Manual employees can achieve maximum earnings relatively early in their careers. Once apprenticeships are completed, craftsmen command the full rate, whilst process workers can hit the 'big money' even more quickly. For the rest of their working lives, however, these individuals' careers offer no automatic increments. Once they are into their twenties, manual workers' earnings have settled on a plateau from which they can be edged up only through overtime, shiftwork and piece-rate schemes. The plateau itself can be raised only through collective action by the bargaining group to which an individual belongs. Blue-collar workers are not devoid of personal ambition; it is circumstances that require an emphasis upon group rather than individual mobility. We need look little further to understand trade unionism's appeal amongst manual workers.

Some individuals do hoist themselves by their bootstraps and are proud of their achievements. It is not unknown for craftsmen to break into self-employment, and many have prospered. There are also many managers, though mostly on the lower and middle rungs, who began their careers on the shop floor. But it is simply impossible for most manual workers to follow these illustrious examples. Like the army, industry requires fewer officers than men. Most manual workers must remain manual workers throughout their working lives. This is what the arithmetic of the labour force decrees. Data from the 1971 census, presented in Table 2.1, show that 65 per cent of all male workers are in manual occupations. Women are more likely to be in routine white-collar jobs – secretaries, typists, receptionists and suchlike. Taking both sexes together, 57 per cent of the workforce is in the manual sector. There is clearly no way in which this working class majority could compress itself into the 22 per cent of all jobs in the Registrar General's upper middle class groups. Of all manual workers in 1953, ten years later less than 10 per cent had risen into white-collar jobs.[2] The life-long progressive career is a middle class privilege.

Table 2.1 Occupational distribution of the labour force (in percentages)

Registrar General's social class	Males	Females	Total
1	5	1	4
2	18	17	18
3 Non-manual	12	38	21
3 Manual	38	10	28
4	18	26	21
5	9	8	8

Source. 1971 Census.

One implication of the quickly reached income plateau is that blue-collar living standards are jeopardized during the child-rearing phase of the life-cycle as wives relinquish employment and children arrive to grow into increasingly expensive dependents[3] White-collar salary progression cushions the effects of these changes in domestic circumstances.

In middle age, when white-collar incomes are peaking, blue-collar earnings actually taper. Physical capacities decline, and with diminishing family responsibilities there is less need to endure overtime, shiftwork and whatever jobs carry the highest earnings. Manual households' standards of life rarely decline into poverty at this stage in the life-cycle, but middle class middle age offers comforts that are unknown in the working class. Whereas amongst individuals in their twenties there is considerable overlap between blue- and white-collar incomes, amongst male employees in their fifties there is hardly any overlap at all.[4]

Over the lifetime white-collar salaries average out well above blue-collar wage levels. In April 1976 white-collar pay averaged 25 per cent above blue-collar earnings. But this is not the only point at issue. Throughout their careers white-collar employees can expect and experience personal mobility. Particularly if they are men, they gradually ascend to positions carrying higher status, pay and authority. They experience the occupational structure as containing a hierarchy of jobs through which individuals can move, starting from the bottom, towards the summit. The manual worker's lifetime offers a vastly different experience – of immobility. Throughout his career the blue-collar worker realizes that he is most unlikely to join 'them'. 'They' inhabit a different world in branches of the occupational structure to which the manual worker has little hope of access.

Economic security

Since the 1960s white-collar redundancy has been attracting attention proportionate only to its previous rarity. Blue-collar workers remain considerably more exposed to unemployment. In June 1975 manual employees comprised 65 per cent of the male labour force, but 83 per cent of the registered male unemployed. The approximately one-and-a-half million out-of-work in 1977 were mostly individuals normally employed in manual occupations. Older workers, without experience in skilled work, and particularly those suffering from some disability, have the greatest difficulty in finding new jobs and are at risk of spending months, sometimes years, on the dole.[5] Redundancy is more common than is often realized. Studies of blue-collar careers indicate that it is by no means unusual for workers to suffer this indignity several times during their working lives. When cuts in government spending herald fears of teacher redundancies the alarm bells ring. For manual workers it is a part of working life which is often applauded in the press as introducing flexibility into the labour market and shaking out labour from less efficient firms and industries. Of course, blue-collar unions fight redundancies, but must often recognize that it is a losing battle. The (mainly white-collar) jobs where entrants can expect a lifetime's work are very much the exceptions.

During the last twenty years government action has tempered the insecurity that previously afflicted manual occupations. Dockwork has been decasualized, the Contracts of Employment legislation entitles workers to stipulated periods of notice, the Redundancy Payments Act has brought financial compensation for loss of job, whilst the Employment Protection Act of 1975 consolidates protection against arbitrary dismissal and restricts managements' rights to lay-off labour. Yet despite this legislation economic insecurity remains an on-going fact of life amongst large sections of the working class. Many of the new legal rights to protection depend upon length of service, and as it is not unusual for manual workers to change jobs frequently, their security remains minimal. Marsden estimates that only a third of all redundancies attract redundancy pay, and that there are up to a million unpaid redundancies each year.[6] Unfortunately not all employees are aware of their legal rights. Unhappily also there are employers only too prepared to take advantage. In the two years up to 1977 Department of Employment inspectors collected more than £76,000 for employees during their spot-checks in twenty-three selected towns following suspicions that many firms were paying less than the minimum rates stipulated on the recommendation of Wages Councils. The spot-checks uncovered extensive underpayment of workers. For example, in Cardiff more than a quarter of the 293 firms inspected, mainly small cafes, shops, hairdressers, clubs and hotels, were paying beneath the statutory rate.[7] What were the trade unions doing? Small-scale industry where jobs are most marginal remains largely unorganized.

In 1975 Martin Leighton left a solid middle class background and career to make a 'journey into the working class'.[8] For eighteen months he worked in a variety of manual jobs before returning to 'civilization' to tell his story. What makes his story interesting is how frequently he was surprised and shocked by circumstances that life-long manual workers take for granted. For example, '. . . no firm I joined made the least attempt to suggest any prospects to me, to give me any information about themselves. In fact my induction as a new employee was always left entirely to my workmates.' The point is that manual workers do not 'join firms', they simply take jobs. Firms do not enrol blue-collar hands as members of the organization; they are hired to do jobs and remain only as long as the jobs last. When working as a handyman for a building and decorating concern, Leighton discovered how short-lived manual jobs can be. 'Fred and I were made redundant at the same time. It had been obvious for some weeks that the firm was short of new orders. On Tuesday they gave us notice to leave that Friday, hoping that we would accept that as a week's notice. . . .Fear of dismissal is markedly less obvious among working people than the middle class. The working man, particularly in the construction trades, knows how vulnerable he is to shifts of the fortune of his employers, and how dispensable he is.' There are limits to the protection that the law can decree. Who wants to be protected in a non-existent job? Rights whose enforcement would drive a firm out of business make little sense.

The damage inflicted by redundancy is only exceptionally short-lived. Herron studied 2,000 men who were 'unloaded' from Upper Clyde Shipbuilders in 1969–70.[9] Most found work in allied engineering industries, but usually suffered a drop in status and earnings in the process. As Parker has stressed, failure to find a new job at one's former level of skill and earnings can be psychologically as well as financially distressing.[10]

Manual workers learn to cope with insecurity of employment as they adjust to other aspects of working class life. Martin and Fryer studied 'Casterton Mills', a firm that halved its labour force of approximately 2,000 during 1967–8.[11] Few workers had firm ideas about the new jobs they would prefer, and the things individuals said they would look for were rarely related to the jobs they eventually obtained. There was a tendency to 'make do', to take the first job meeting minimum criteria such as not too low paid or totally disagreeable. Strangers to working class culture find this acquiescence remarkable, and these reactions are instructive reminders that manual work is different.

Loss of one's job is an extreme experience and is only one aspect of the manual worker's insecurity. When trade booms, unlimited overtime becomes available. Months later short-time and lay-offs can be threatened. Managements complain of the disruption caused by strikes, and industrial disputes inconvenience shop-floor workers as much as anyone else. For manual workers, however, strikes figure as only one amongst several sources of fluctuating earnings.

As already recognized, some manual workers are well paid by any white-collar standards. The catch is that their affluence is not securely anchored in progressive careers. It is difficult for any manual worker to spend a life-time in well-paid work. Construction workers who are willing to migrate around the country to sites where their skills are in short supply can make money whilst they and their families tolerate the unsettled routine. Jobs on oil-rigs can be remunerative, but who would recommend a life-time on them? Work in extreme conditions such as constructing underground transport systems has to be well paid to be accomplished, but few individuals are capable of meeting the physical demands for a lifetime. Manual workers are exposed to the greatest risks of physical injury at work. There are over 2,000 industrial fatalities each year and few occur in offices.[12] The dangers of coal-mining are well-known, but many factories are also dangerous and unhealthy places.

Michael Lane has described how the world of the white-collar worker tends to be a secure and predictable place.[13] It makes sense to plan ahead, to think of tomorrow and to invest, in education and training for example, to reap longer-term gains. In contrast, the blue-collar worker's world is uncertain. His job and income are never secure. Lane argues that the working class habit of living for today is better regarded as a rational adjustment to circumstance than the source of economic difficulties. It was once hoped that the welfare state would make genuine social security into a right of citizenship, and the state's safety-net does avert the extreme poverty of the 1930s and before. Yet unless individuals' normal earnings fail to lift them clear of the official poverty line, dependence upon state social security still means a fall in living standards. Unemployment and sickness mean financial hardship in working class families. Redundancy payments average hundreds rather than thousands of pounds and do not rival directors' golden handshakes. State retirement pensions lag well behind average wage levels. An impoverished old age is not an attractive prospect, but it is one of the near-certainties that millions of manual workers can anticipate. The middle classes are served by 'the other welfare state' whose beneficiaries are rarely labelled scroungers. In addition to relative security of employment and stability of earnings, white-collar jobs tend to be surrounded by a system of fringe benefits far superior to anything available to the working class. Time off work to visit doctors and dentists rarely entails loss of earnings, full pay during periods of sickness is standard, and occupational pensions are realistically related to normal earnings. In higher level managerial and professional employment there are further perks like private health insurance, use of company vehicles and expense accounts. In addition, at this level a further branch of the other welfare state comes into operation; the provisions whereby mortgage interest payments, insurance premiums and a variety of expenses can be offset against income tax liability. The majority of manual workers derive scant benefit from these social services.[14]

In 1968 Wedderburn and Craig collected information from a national sample of manufacturing firms about the conditions of work applying to male employees with over five years' service aged between thirty-five and forty but in different occupations.[15] Some of the inequalities revealed between the treatment of shop-floor operatives and those on the lowest, clerical level of white-collar employment were dramatic. For example, operatives in only 38 per cent of the firms were entitled to over 15 days holiday (excluding public holidays) per year, whilst clerical workers enjoyed this entitlement in 74 per cent. Choice of holiday time was available for clerks in 76 per cent of the concerns as against 35 per cent for operatives. Ninety-seven per cent of the firms had a working week for operatives in excess of 40 hours but only 7 per cent for clerks. Ninety per cent adjusted operatives' pay for lateness whereas only 8 per cent subjected clerical workers to this sanction. These inequalities may cause few white-collar workers to feel over-privileged, but it is understandable if they help manual workers to realize their position as a distinct working class.

The sale of labour power

For manual employees work equals the sale of labour power. At least this is a dominant feature of employment. It is a characteristic of work that the non-manual strata often find difficult to grasp since it is so alien to their own experience. White-collar employees rarely sell pure labour power. There are real senses in which they become partners or members of the organizations in which they work. Managers and professional people are not offered mere jobs; they have careers which often involve a prolonged commitment from an employer. Whereas manual labour is commonly bought by the hour, the non-manual worker is offered closer integration into the organization. The generous fringe benefits are symptoms of this integration. The middle classes take this status for granted but manual work is different. In manual occupations the worker is dispensable; it is his labour power that the employer purchases.

One of Martin Leighton's surprises during his journey into the working class was the absence of the numerous perks that the middle classes learn to expect. 'It came as a shock to realise that our breaks for lunch and tea were not part of our hours worked, that we worked a nine-hour shift for eight hours pay. We had no privileges: if we stretched a tea break we "stole" it, if we had to take the wife to hospital or go to the dentist we lost hours and pay. Our lower status was assumed; facilities were primitive, lavatories less hygienic, soap cheaper.' There are many aspects to the closer integration of the white collar worker. On a material level there are the fringe benefits in which employers recognize that apart from being a worker the salaried employee is also a person who occasionally needs time off to handle domestic problems, an income during periods of sickness and security following retirement. It is recognized that he will welcome physically attractive conditions of work, clean toilets and canteen facilities.

Needless to say, these privileges are not offered without expectation of return. Integration through the provision of benefits encourages normative integration; a perception of a harmony of interests between employer and employee. The integration of the salaried employee into the organization involves reciprocal rights and responsibilities. In larger concerns he is expected to be an organization or corporation man. In smaller firms he is expected to display personal loyalty to the employer. Rather than mere labour, the salaried employee is expected to sell a part of his 'self'. Directors, managers and salesmen must identify with their companies, or at least appear to do so. They have to represent their organizations to clients and customers and, equally important, they are entrusted to mediate its demands to blue-collar subordinates. White-collar workers are entrusted with discretion and authority. In contrast, to use Alan Fox's terminology, the blue-collar employment relationship is 'low-trust'.[16] Employers do not expect workers to offer anything beyond labour power. In return, employees expect little reward beyond the pay-packet. The approach of both parties to the employment relationship is calculative with the cash nexus well-exposed. To the firm, labour is a cost of production to be kept as low as possible in exchange for as much output as practical, whilst for their part workers seek to maximize the returns on their labour. The above comments are obviously exaggerations. There are routine white-collar jobs where conditions of work are proletarian, just as there are thousands of blue-collar workers for whom employment is something more than the sale of crude labour power. As generalizations, however, the staff–works contrasts drawn above are valid.

Non-manual workers in general bring not only labour power to their jobs; they have motivation, skill and knowledge, the products of education and training, to place at employers' disposal. There are skilled manual workers who used to be called an aristocracy of labour, but even their skills are normally acquired on-the-job under the ultimate supervision of employers. Whilst the practice of certain manual occupations including the printing and shipyard trades is regulated by the craft-groups, resulting in a style of management sometimes called 'craft administration', the employer remains the judge of the quality and value of the product. Professional employment is different. In the professions the acquisition of esoteric expertise, knowledge and skill are not controlled by employers. In a professional – client relationship, the buyer is deemed unqualified to judge the value of the services rendered. Only a professional's equally qualified peers are considered competent judges. Skill and know-how are bought 'on trust' which allows considerable discretion. This is unlike the sale of albeit sometimes skilled labour power which the employer then uses in ways and towards ends that he determines.

When Marxists discuss the alienation of the worker they are not only drawing attention to the monotony of jobs created by an advanced division of labour: they are pinpointing a more pervasive malaise. The worker is estranged from the product of his labour and his tools, which are the property of the employer, and from his own labour power which also becomes the employer's property for an agreed number of hours, to be used in ways that can violate the worker's true nature. Today labour power is rarely extracted and controlled with the boss at the elbow. More insidious forms of control are available. Technology can control both the pace and quality of work. Piece-rate and bonus schemes operate not only as incentives but also as continuous checks on productivity. The organization of work in industry is characterized by a distinction between conception and execution. Work is planned and controlled in the office. Manual work is the muscle that enacts plans conceived elsewhere. People in white-collar jobs may feel that distinguishing the worker from his labour power is abstract hair-splitting. As a result of their own experience, manual workers find it easier to see the point.

The working class is often berated for its irresponsibility. The unofficial striker has become a folk-devil. To their even greater cost, managements are conscious of a problem of motivation. In industry it is everyday knowledge that an infusion of goodwill and effort could boost production without any increase in capital or labour costs. Unfortunately the workers are bloody-minded. They remain addicted to their tea-breaks, visits to the toilet and restrictive practices. Managements like to believe that they have done nothing to deserve such resistance. Some are making genuine attempts to motivate their workers and try to treat them like real human beings. In point of fact, however, the culture of workplace resistance which can also involve pilfering and turning a blind-eye to acts of sabotage, has evolved over generations as a response to the nature of manual work. We should not be surprised at this culture's capacity to overwhelm managements' palliatives. Fox argues that '. . .work for the majority is little more than an irksome precondition for the real business of living'.[17] What is more, it is industrialism that has taught the working class that the predominant meaning of work is instrumental. 'Generations of the working class, subjected to this pattern of work experience, have made a "realistic" adaptation to it by relinquishing, or by never bothering to take seriously, aspirations towards intrinsic satisfactions.'[18]

The manner in which factory jobs are subdivided and controlled is sometimes presented as a 'technological imperative'. Managers and owners disclaim responsibility for conditions on their shopfloors. Technology decrees how work must be organized. Like everyone else, managers and owners have to accommodate to the technological facts of life. Another view labels the above ideas as ideological. Existing technologies have developed within definite socio-economic relations and reflect the dominant interests. Presenting technology as neutral simply masks the system of domination. Is it surprising if workers are less enthusiastic than managements in cooperatively adapting to the received facts of industrial life?

Job satisfaction

Job satisfaction is a difficult concept to operationalize. Whether it can be measured and, if so how, are matters of debate. Can a question such as, 'How satisfied are you with your job?' hope to tap individuals' real feelings? The very term 'satisfaction' is ambiguous. Is the question enquiring whether a job is satisfying or satisfactory? In a society where the belief reigns that individuals are responsible for choosing their own jobs, can individuals be expected to confess dissatisfaction? Many investigators prefer to break the job satisfaction concept down to probe individuals' assessments of their pay, prospects, security, working conditions and so on. Others make alienation the central concept and enquire whether employees feel powerless, bored and estranged from their fellow workers. There are numerous approaches to measuring the quality of working life, but whatever the measuring technique, in general manual workers score lower than white-collar employees, and this finding has been consistently repeated through decades of research.

Motor vehicle assembly lines are much studied because they represent an extreme case.[19] There are few opportunities for job satisfaction on the assembly track. The work is monotonous with job cycles often lasting less than a minute. In addition the work is physically arduous. The track carries vehicles along with unremitting regularity, whilst jobs can involve handling heavy equipment and manoeuvring in physically exacting positions. The cheers that ring when the track breaks down demonstrate the workers' feelings. What is more, it is difficult for the individual worker to associate his particular job with the eventual product. Assembly-line workers cannot regard themselves as car-makers.

No one pretends that motor vehicle assembly is a typical manual occupation. Nevertheless, it illustrates the deprivations to which manual workers are generally subject, admittedly to different degrees, compared with their white-collar counterparts. Most manual jobs may not arouse constant feelings of boredom but, at the same time, the work rarely operates as a central life interest.[20] When asked to consider a situation of a genuine free choice, such as following a pools win, only a minority of manual workers express a preference for continuing in the same or similar jobs. Some researchers consider the question, 'What work would you try to get into if you could start all over again?' a particularly sensitive indicator of individuals' attachments to their occupations, and the proportions naming their own jobs steadily decline as the hierarchy is descended. University professors, lawyers, scientists and journalists all show percentages over 80, the majority of manual workers choose different occupations, and of unskilled carworkers only 16 per cent name their own jobs.[21]

Middle class spiralists pursue careers which often take them around the country as they progress upwards, and mostly consider the dislocation to home and community life acceptable.[22] The rewards that accompany middle class careers justify the sacrifices. In contrast, the majority of manual workers believe that no job they could conceivably be offered would justify leaving friends and kinfolk. In their enquiries into labour mobility in Britain, Harris and Clausen found that 57 per cent of their respondents argued they could envisage no economic circumstances whatsoever that might persuade them to move to another part of the United Kingdom.[23] Likewise, following the redundancies at 'Casterton Mills', Martin and Fryer discovered that nearly every individual insisted on remaining local.[24]

Factory workers adjust their aspirations to reality. Children from working class homes are less likely than middle class peers to aspire to enter intrinsically satisfying jobs.[25] In working class circles it is recognized that the major rewards from work will be financial. There is some debate as to the possibility of manual employees 'compensating' for their less satisfying working lives during leisure.[26] One school of thought alleges that monotonous work so stultifies the personality as to reduce the likelihood of creative interests.[27] But even if compensation were possible, the fact would remain that manual work is relatively devoid of intrinsic interest. The fact that manual jobs are physically exacting also deserves some stress. Even 'light' assembly work takes its toll during an eight-hour shift. Leisure research shows that manual workers watch more television than individuals in white-collar occupations. Why do they waste time so passively? One reason concerns the need to physically recuperate from work, and it is also relevant that on average blue-collar employees work eight or nine hours longer than the thirty-five hour week that is now normal for staff. Whilst their average earnings were only 25 per cent in excess of blue-collar levels, in 1976 white-collar workers were earning 46 per cent more per hour.

Prestige

Status and esteem are such nebulous commodities that their importance is easily dismissed. Who cares whether others look up or down? In practice we all do, and all the research shows that manual work is held in low esteem. There is some overlap between the prestige attached to skilled manual and the more routine white-collar jobs, but non-skilled blue-collar occupations are unambiguously at the bottom of the heap.[28] Matters are a trifle more complicated than this suggests. There is not total agreement throughout the public on the prestige attached to different occupations, and even less on the prestige that these occupations merit.[29] All groups tend to upgrade their own and similar jobs. Skilled workers accentuate the importance of their work, whilst individuals in business tend to emphasize the merit of all industrial occupations. In a sample of 100 working class men from London's East End, Willmott and Young discovered 22 'deviants' who inverted the conventional hierarchy and placed manual occupations at the top.[30] But even these dissenters know that they live in a society where little esteem is attached to their own jobs.

This matters because an individual's job is part of his social persona. As Everet Hughes has observed, '. . .a man's work is one of the things by which he is judged, and certainly one of the more significant things by which he judges himself . . . A man's work is one of the more important parts of his social identity, of his self; indeed, of his fate in the one life he has to live, for there is something almost as irrevocable about choice of occupation as there is about choice of a mate.'[31] We place each other with reference to our occupations. The getting acquainted question, 'What do you do?' is ordinarily taken to mean 'What work?' and we treat our fellows differently depending on their jobs. Controlled research in street situations, where actors dressed to represent different classes ask passers-by the time, shows that responses vary.[32]

People learn who they are. Doctors are not constantly surprised at the respect with which they are treated. Likewise manual workers feel little affront at their repeated denial of status. This fact of working class life only makes its full impact upon a stranger such as Martin Leighton, who spent a spell as a roadsweeper during his working class journey. 'As for myself, I was all too keenly aware of the social status my job conferred on me. I had become a non-person. People simply did not see me any longer: I felt that, but for the physical problem of mass, they would have walked through me.' This is one of the 'hidden injuries of class' that Sennett and Cobb deplore.[33] Their long interviews with working people in Boston USA yielded plentiful evidence of how menial jobs devalue the worker. In our society people are judged by their jobs, by what they produce, and the value of their labour is crudely measured in the market place. This is what a person essentially 'is'. Hence the ability of low-status jobs to devalue workers' selves. Kohn and Schooler have shown that the psychological effects of work are anything but trivial.[34] Qualities associated with jobs are carried into non-working life. Jobs that demand simple obedience encourage workers to demand this quality of their children. Berger illustrates how work that is specialized to the point of being meaningless denies a person any credible conception of himself.[35] Manual workers learn to live with all this. Directors who pretend that everyone is working class are simply concealing from themselves what others endure.

What is a manual worker?

It is impossible to offer concise yet satisfactory definitions of terms such as blue-collar and manual.[36] The expressions cannot be taken literally. In these days of denim fashions, blue-collars are evident elsewhere than on factory floors, whilst nearly all jobs require some combination of manual and mental effort. What is remarkable is that despite their literal imprecision, the manual and white-collar concepts remain in everyday use and rarely create misunderstandings. This is because the concepts draw attention to a very real distinction between different types of occupations, but one which results from the manner in which a syndrome of rewards and deprivations cluster, rather than the operation of any single factor.

Manual work is the sale of labour power, little more, for money and little else. It offers no prospects of a progressive career and little security. The incumbent remains constantly on the receiving end of authority. If the work is intrinsically satisfying, this is an unexpected bonus, not a normal expectation. By the public-at-large the work is accorded little status. Of course, there are jobs that possess some of these features but not others. Is shop-work manual or non-manual? There are ambiguous cases, but the vast majority of jobs are clearly on one side of the divide or the other, and most workers know where they stand.

It is not alien socialist propaganda that encourages the majority of manual workers to identify with the working class. It is rather the everyday experience of selling their labour to 'them' – who work in relatively congenial conditions, enjoy security, exercise authority and have the prospect of careers leading to wealth beyond the bounds of possibility for ordinary working men. Manual workers realize how remote their chances are of saying goodbye to the working class. Higher pay and greater security, if available at all, must be won for the class to which manual workers already belong. Hence their support for trade unions and the Labour Party which promise the best chance of redistributing privilege in favour of the working class. This working class culture, in which individual workers are immersed to varying extents, is a response to the brute facts of life for manual workers.

Is manual work being upgraded?

One body of opinion argues that whilst the above analysis was valid in the past, it is becoming decreasingly true to life. It is claimed that manual work is changing and being upgraded in the process, closing the old staff–works rift, thereby giving manual workers less reason to consider themselves a class apart, and leaving the overall system of stratification bearing a closer resemblance to the continuous scale postulated by functionalists. There are several versions of this argument and the account below is a synoptic gloss.[37] The argument draws attention, firstly, to technological trends which, it is claimed, are reducing the demand for elementary muscle power and requiring greater technical competence of the labour force. It is argued that as more jobs are mechanized, demand for unskilled labour declines whilst demand for skilled workers increases. They may not be craftsmen in the traditional sense but they are required to be technically competent and responsible, capable of operating and maintaining sophisticated capital equipment. Hence the commonplace emphasis on the need for a more highly educated work-force. Blauner has argued that the assembly line is just an intermediate stage in technological advance which will be progressively superceded by the automated factory.[38] In such establishments work is not physically arduous. It consists of maintaining and supervising equipment that accomplishes the routine of production automatically. Work-groups can be given discretion, responsibility and variety in their work. Close supervision has no place in the automated plant, and rather than appendages, the workers become masters of machinery. Alienation will be replaced by freedom, according to Blauner's optimistic forecast.

Secondly, the upgrading theory draws attention to the decline of small workshops and the movement of labour into large corporations which can offer greater security of employment. Equally important, enlightened personnel departments are seen as abandoning the orthodoxies of scientific management – the sub-division of work into easily learnt jobs, the stop-watch of work-study and piece-rate incentives. Experts in human relations proclaim the virtues of participation, democratic leadership, autonomous work-groups, job enrichment and job enlargement. Optimists point to a spate of books and articles on the quality of working life,[39] in which researchers highlight the possibilities of job-redesign and managers listen with approval. Hence the scenario of manual workers being accorded the treatment to integrate them into and foster identification with their companies.

Thirdly, the theory argues that the above technological and organizational trends are widening genuine career opportunities for blue-collar workers. In large organizations manual jobs can be arranged hierarchically, enabling recruits to move towards technician and supervisory levels. The trends towards manual workers being accorded the formalities of salaried status – being paid monthly and by cheque, are seen as symptomatic of how things are moving. Fourthly, attention is drawn to the impact of government policies. Post-Keynesian macro-economic management allied to social security and employment legislation has lessened the insecurity formerly associated with blue-collar work. Fifthly, the rise of trade unionism is claimed to have produced a more even balance of power in industry. Employers' rights to hire and fire have been curbed, whilst middle class fringe benefits are increasingly negotiated on behalf of blue-collar workers. Holidays with pay, for example, finally ceased to be a middle class privilege between the world wars, but as recently as 1960 few manual workers had more than a fortnight's entitlement in addition to public holidays. Today three and four weeks are common. Meanwhile there has been no contraction of the work-year for groups whose holiday entitlement has traditionally been generous including teachers and senior civil servants. The gap has been closing.

Individually all the above trends could be dismissed as insignificant. Collectively it is argued that they amount to an upgrading of blue-collar work. No one claims that these trends are benefitting all manual workers to the same extent, but it is suggested that the section affected will become sufficiently large to obliterate the traditional break between white- and blue-collar employment. It is anticipated that trade unionism will cease to be a working class movement; that unions will become organizations representing the diverse interests of groups in both white- and blue-collar occupations. Another envisaged effect is a declining relationship between individuals' jobs and their subjective class identities.[40] In politics the expected trend is away from 'class' reasons for voting, leading to greater deviance from traditional class norms and parties appealing across traditional class lines. Some commentators claim to read all these trends in current events.

This is an appropriate point to stress how difficult it always is to appraise theories about the direction of change over time. It is exceptionally good fortune when earlier generations of social scientists turn out to have collected the information we would now like to have available to test theories currently being expounded. In the case of the upgrading theory we simply do not possess the longitudinal data that a thorough test would require. What we do possess are the results of recent studies conducted in the light of the theory's claims, and this evidence is consistently contrary to the view that manual work is losing its working class character. Firstly, detailed studies in particular companies suggest that, even collectively, the changes to which the upgrading theory draws attention are too marginal to make any real difference to the class situation of the manual worker. One of the best examples is Theo Nichols' enquiry which involved over three years' observation and interviewing at a southern England site of 'ChemCo', a large organization with branches throughout Britain. Nichols investigated the labour force at ChemCo which was neither militant, nor completely docile, and, more significantly for the present argument, the ChemCo management was also studied.[41] On the surface management appeared progressive and enlightened. Motivating the men on the shop-floor was perceived as a problem to which management enthusiastically brought the vocabulary of human relations. ChemCo acknowledged the virtues of employee participation, job enrichment and job enlargement. Following three years' research, however, Nichols labelled the managerial style as 'mock socialism'. Actual changes in the plant were less impressive than the jargon. Job rotation, for example, usually meant doing three boring jobs per shift instead of one. Nichols argues that, given the manner in which the economy is organized, measures to enhance the quality of working life cannot be pushed to the point where they would interfere with managerial control and profitability. He also disputes allegations that marginal concessions from management might be the spark to ignite more militant shop-floor demands for workers' control.[42] At ChemCo there were no signs of such developments.

Following a survey of the relevant literature, Alan Fox has endorsed the view that the overall logic of the economic system militates against fundamental improvements in the quality of working life.[43] Fox suggests that managements become interested in this problem only when the quest for output and profit has been pushed to such extremes that effort and morale sag, whilst labour turnover, disputes and absenteeism increase. Not even the most progressive managements are bent upon reorganizing work in accordance with new principles. The management of work remains primarily instrumental; profitable turnover rather than humane experience is the over-riding objective. Kelly's review of the Glacier project points to a similar conclusion.[44] Since the 1940s, the Glacier Company has earned renown as an avant-garde organization, anxious to apply fashionable ideas, and has cooperated with social scientists in monitoring a series of action research projects. However, Kelly's review of these projects over a period of more than twenty years reveals that ideas have been taken up and dropped as occasioned by commercial convenience. No one argues that manual work is exactly the same as in the 1930s. Holidays are longer and payment by cheque more common. These and other trends have provoked the upgrading theorists into action. But are the changes really as momentous as the theories? The most detailed recent studies of industrial work invite scepticism.

A second set of enquiries has bolstered parallel doubts as to whether the changes in manual work to which the upgrading theory draws attention really have the suggested implications for workers' attitudes. Michael Mann investigated the labour force at Birds (coffee and custard) plant during its relocation over forty-two miles from Birmingham to Banbury in the mid-1960s.[45] The bulk of the thousand-plus work-force chose to move with the company. Why? Other jobs were available within reach of their homes. Management presented the move favourably and offered inducements. Equally important, the workers had achieved positions in the firm that they were reluctant to abandon. Their earnings were relatively secure and high compared with wage levels in other firms. Also, during their employment with the company, longer serving workers had achieved promotion to higher-paid jobs and had become entitled to fringe benefits including pensions, longer holidays and sick pay. On the surface this evidence seems consistent with the view of manual work being upgraded, opening career opportunities and integrating employees into the organization. However, Mann's interviews with the workers suggested a different interpretation. Mann described the Birds' labour force as 'employment dependent'. They had achieved positions in the company's internal labour market that offered more favourable opportunities than those available externally. Hence their employment dependence. At the same time, the workers neither identified with the company nor obtained the intrinsic job satisfactions characteristic in white-collar work. Attitudes towards work and the firm remained fundamentally instrumental. The workers were continuing to sell their labour in the most advantageous market.

Cotgrove's study of *The Nylon Spinners*[46] offers further evidence of the capacity of manual workers' attitudes to remain typically working class. This study monitored a productivity agreement that allowed not only for increased pay, but also changes in work organization involving job enlargement and less supervision. From the company's point of view the package was successful; productivity rose and labour turnover fell. For this discussion, however, it is the workers' responses to the changes that are interesting. The spinners' assessments of the deal were overwhelmingly favourable. Morale improved and workers reported that their jobs had become more interesting. But the main attraction of the agreement, and the main perceived benefit, was the increased pay. For the labour force in this plant, attachments to work remained primarily instrumental. Work continued to be the sale of labour for money. Once again, there was little evidence of middle class orientations such as stressing intrinsic job satisfactions and identifying with the organisation.

Wedderburn and Crompton's research at the 'Seagrass' works is also relevant.[47] This was a continuous process plant and the enquiry confirmed previous suggestions that an automated technology engenders relatively favourable job attitudes. At the same time, instrumental orientations remained predominant, and Wedderburn and Crompton emphasize how volatile these orientations can be. *The Affluent Worker* enquiry,[48] which will be discussed in the next chapter, had stressed the possibility of a harmony of interests between instrumentally oriented workers and successful firms capable of offering high rates of pay. The 'Seagrass' enquiry, however, revealed that satisfaction with pay can change considerably over short periods as a result of wage movements in other firms and industries. Instrumental orientations do not attach blue-collar workers to their jobs in a manner comparable with the integration of non-manual employees. All the relevant enquiries suggest that even in large progressive companies using advanced technology, manual workers' attitudes remain distinctly working class.

There is a diametrically opposed view which, in contrast to the upgrading theory, argues that a progressive degradation of manual work is occurring. Braverman is amongst this degradation argument's most forceful exponents,[49] claiming that the principles of scientific management with their emphasis on the sub-division of tasks and use of economic incentives may have lost favour amongst social scientists but continue to flourish amongst line managers and work study engineers. Personnel specialists have learnt the language of human relations, but in industry their role is confined to treating the discontent that mainline management arouses. Braverman argues that the real trends are towards a de-skilling of manual work, nominally skilled trades have ceased to involve craftsmanship in the traditional sense. Skill is constantly transferred from workers' hands to machines and destroyed by the specialized division of labour, whilst control of work processes is increasingly appropriated by managements. The major currents of organizational and technological development, in Braverman's view, make for a more systematic exploitation of the working class.

Braverman focuses upon the losses whereas upgrading theorists rivet attention on the gains flowing to the blue-collar labour force. The golden mean is not always valid, but in this case the truth probably does lie between the extremes. Machines may have taken skill from craftsmen's hands, but they have also taken much of the brute labour out of non-skilled manual work. Chadwick-Jones' research in the tinning section of the steel industry, conducted over six years during the change-over from batch to continuous process technology, offers an unusually balanced account of the gains and losses for the manual labour force.[50] Following the changes the workers were more satisfied with their (higher) pay and improved working conditions, and spoke approvingly of how their work had become less physically arduous. At the same time, they regretted the decline of the old work-group spirit and the new separation between employee and supervisory levels. In other industries the balance sheet from organizational and technological developments will read differently, but it is doubtful whether an aggregated impression would justify talk of a wholesale degradation of manual work. At the same time, as we have seen, there is scant evidence to support the view that a substantial number of blue-collar occupations are losing the characteristics traditionally associated with manual employment.

If the boundary above the working class is shifting, a more likely cause is the proletarianization of routine white-collar work.[51] Trends in electoral behaviour suggest that individuals in the least prestigious white-collar occupations are becoming increasingly proletarian in outlook,[52] and these are the political consequences that changes in the organization of white-collar work lead us to anticipate. In place of the traditional personal relationship with the boss, in large modern corporations shop-floor conditions are being introduced in secretarial pools, drawing offices, laboratories and machine rooms. Graduates and other professionally qualified recruits enter organizations overhead, creating a promotion blockage for entrants at the foot of the white-collar hierarchy. In terms of career prospects, pay levels, opportunities for intrinsic job satisfaction and prestige, the routine white-collar employee is losing his former advantages vis-à-vis the works. His job is becoming working class, and attitudes appear to be changing accordingly.

Analysing the position of the white-collar worker in the class structure runs beyond the scope of this volume. For present purposes, it is sufficient to note that if a trend towards proletarianization is underway, it will not obliterate the boundary above the working class. It will merely shift the line upwards to encompass certain occupations whose incumbents formerly dissociated themselves from manual workers. The latter's treatment at work has laid the bedrock for a distinctly working class culture, and there is little evidence of this bedrock crumbling.

Socio-economic trends: 3
is the working class in decline?

Overturned differentials; folk-myth or fact?

The overtaken white-collar worker has become a well-known figure. It is part of current received 'knowledge' that traditional pay differentials have been compressed and in some cases upturned. Manual workers, particularly those in strong trade unions, have been seen as forging up the pay league. During periods of pay restraint we constantly hear about the erosion of middle managers' differentials, and supervisors whose take-home pay is exceeded by subordinates. White-collar workers, formerly restrained by status consciousness or a professional ideal of service, are seen as belatedly turning to trade unionism and, in some instances, militant tactics, in a vain attempt to stem the tide. Unhappily for them, the middle classes usually discover that they lack the 'muscle' to cause a rapid and embarrassing loss of output by withdrawing their labour. Teachers and branch bank clerks can strike for months without the balance of payments suffering or a chain reaction of lay-offs. White-collar employees complain of unfair treatment by government pay policies that are tuned to sweeten unions on whose support the success of economic strategies and governments' survival can depend. Not only are their interests neglected in the letter of pay codes, but employees on salaries find it difficult to bend the rules in ways that, they suspect, are possible when earnings depend upon piece-rates, bonuses and a multitude of additional allowances. For many people the fall of the Heath government during the coal-miners' strike in 1974 crudely pinpointed the new centre of economic power. If they climb towards the top of career ladders, striving managers and professional workers feel cheated by progressive income tax. Hence the emigration scares. We are warned that Britain will be drained of her best brains. Eminent doctors and scientists who depart for better paid jobs abroad provoke concern for a whole stratum of white-collar workers trapped between avaricious blue-collar unions on the one hand, and government pay and tax policies on the other.

Despite its prevalence there is little hard evidence to support this folk-lore. It is necessary to distinguish short- from long-term trends. For brief periods particular occupations can do exceptionally well in the pay rounds. At the time of the 'Houghton award' in the mid-1970s teaching became an attractively paid occupation. Throughout the 1960s car workers were renowned for their affluence, but by the late 1970s motor vehicle assembly had ceased to be particularly well paid. Since decasualization in the 1960s, dockworkers have enjoyed above-average earnings, but live in the shadow of redundancy in an industry with a declining labour force. Forty years ago workers in transport were envied. Jobs on the buses, trams and railways were much sought on account of their decent and, most important, secure earnings. Over the longer term the most impressive feature of pay differentials has been their stability, and some white-collar groups including managers are amongst the exceptions who have made significant gains.[1] On average non-manual employees still enjoy the higher earnings. During their lifetimes university graduates can expect to earn more than twice as much as individuals who leave full-time education at the earliest opportunity.

An overlap between blue- and white-collar earnings is not novel. In the nineteenth century elementary school teachers earned no more than artisans.[2] Likewise the counting house clerk did not enjoy a superior income compared with skilled labour.[3] White-collar workers had other advantages including holidays, security and sometimes pensions. Then there were status distinctions; the middle classes were usually better educated and dressed differently for work. In so far as the superior standing of white-collar work has evaporated it is these other differentials rather than pay that have been eroded. Some contemporary comparisons between blue- and white-collar earnings are grossly misleading. Beginning teachers and junior hospital doctors can point to manual workers whose take-home pay is higher. What is sometimes forgotten is that junior doctors and teachers have incremental salary scales and career ladders to climb. Furthermore, the routine and lower-paid white-collar grades are filled mainly by women. Sex discrimination in employment is now illegal, but up to and including the present the use of women to operate telephones, duplicators, typewriters and filing cabinets has enhanced the career prospects of male employees.

How can we account for the widespread belief in the overtaken white-collar worker? Surveys repeatedly indicate that this folklore is widespread and, correct or not, all beliefs are liable to be real in their consequences. In the 1960s Runciman found the majority amongst a national sample of white-collar workers agreeing that, on average, blue-collar employees had become better paid.[4] Likewise our 1972 fieldwork in Liverpool revealed the majority of non-manual respondents talking of how white- and blue-collar pay differentials had narrowed, and constantly naming manual groups as having made the greatest gains in recent pay rises.[5] Studies of white-collar unionists have shown that their support for trade unionism is often based on a reluctant militancy, fuelled by the feeling that they are lagging behind.[6]

Manual pay increases tend to be negotiated and announced in ways that make a maximum impact. The conferences of the major unions are conducted before a national audience informed through broadcasts and press reports. The progress of actual pay negotiations that directly affect thousands of workers, as in the coal industry, is reported daily through the media and eventual settlements are announced to the nation. White-collar pay rises tend to be surrounded by less publicity. The exceptions mostly concern public employees – civil servants, local government officers, teachers and doctors. In these cases large unions negotiate on the national stage with all the attendant publicity, and this has no doubt contributed to the impression of employees in the public sector as feather-bedded. In private industry managers' pay rises tend to be handed out quietly behind the scenes. In 1970 the process workers at Pilkingtons in St Helens were involved in a seven-week-long and highly publicized unofficial strike that secured a £3 increase on gross rates of pay, an increase that was subsequently applied not only to those who took industrial action but to all employees in the company including managers.[7] There is evidence of bias in media reports on industrial relations. Managements tend to be treated on the assumption that they have 'reasonable' cases to offer; shop-floor grievances are viewed as reflecting sectional rather than national interests.[8] It is also the case that many middle class interest groups have become skilled in the arts of efficient and articulate organization whilst retaining a 'reasonable' image. During 1975–7 the plights of managers whose pay rises were both limited by prevailing pay codes and decimated by direct taxation were paraded daily. Less was heard about blue-collar workers who were unable to secure the maximum increases that pay norms permitted. Little was also heard about the manual workers whose earnings did not lift them above the minimum considered necessary by the Supplementary Benefits Commission but were nevertheless subject to income tax.

Blue-collar workers are not driving ahead wholesale. However, rather than simply debunking the folk-lore, sociology needs to ask why it succeeds in sounding plausible. A possible explanation concerns the manner in which rising working class standards of living since the 1950s have interacted with other trends. A range of formerly middle class privileges have either been eroded or transformed into universal rights. For example, the 1944 Education Act and, possibly to an even greater extent, the advent of comprehensive secondary schools, have removed the more naked educational privileges that middle class families formerly enjoyed. Likewise urban redevelopment and the mass creation of both council and owner-occupied suburban estates has allowed the working class to escape from inner-city ghettoes. The welfare state has made pensions and sick pay into universal rights. Office automation and company mergers have led to white-collar redundancies, whilst the relatively full employment from 1945 to the 1970s brought greater security to manual workers. Pay is a highly visible and negotiable indicator of a group's position in the social hierarchy. Studies of industrial unrest have shown that a variety of 'background' grievances are often expressed through pay demands.[9] A pay increase is an objective upon which all workers in a bargaining group can unite whatever their particular grievances. It is also an issue on which managements and governments can be persuaded at least to negotiate. It is possible, therefore, that the middle class feeling of being overtaken is a response to the erosion of a broader spectrum of socio-economic differentials. Likewise, even if their wages have not out-distanced salary levels, it is possible that the position of manual workers in the class structure has changed as a result of a wider pattern of socio-economic developments.

A sociological statement: incongruence

As stated in the opening chapter, one of sociology's ways of analysing inequality is to adopt a multi-dimensional perspective, distinguishing the various resources that people value. Income is unequally distributed, likewise with occupational prestige and educational success, whilst houses and districts vary in desirability. Individuals can be ranked along each of these separable dimensions, and whilst overall the rank orders correlate positively, instances of incongruence or inconsistency do occur. Wealthy persons tend to enjoy high incomes, to be well educated, live in superior houses and so on. But there are (a few) university graduates in manual occupations, and some fairly prestigious jobs like minister of religion are not always well paid.

Status inconsistency has attracted sociological interest, with one theory alleging that individuals in ambiguous circumstances will feel anxious and insecure, liable to become social isolates or supporters of authoritarian political movements that promise to restore certainty and order. However, in this discussion the theory that concerns us is one alleging an overall trend away from previously higher levels of congruence. It is argued that, in the past, numerous types of inequality hung together so as to distinguish clearly the middle and working classes. Manual workers received an inferior education, lived in cheaper rented property, worked longer hours in less secure and generally lower-paid jobs; circumstances that coalesced to produce a distinctly working class culture incorporating its own life-styles and values. Over time it is claimed that resources are becoming distributed in decreasingly congruent ways. Even if, as argued in the last chapter, manual work itself is not losing its essential character and still lacks the prestige of white-collar employment, it remains possible to draw attention to workers who are sometimes not only as well paid as individuals in office jobs, but have often achieved middle class levels of educational success by passing secondary school exams and gaining higher qualifications through evening classes and day-release at technical colleges. From their new affluent economic base, it has been argued, blue-collar households today are emulating middle class life-styles in suburban semis with wall-to-wall carpets, and the net result is seen as differences of occupation, income, status and life-style ceasing to coalesce to produce a clear break or division of interest between the working and middle classes. It could be these trends that encourage many white-collar workers to feel that the rungs on the class structure upon which they used to be securely anchored have been pulled from under their feet. According to this interpretation, the emergent class structure possesses a diamond-like contour. Large sections of both the manual and non-manual strata are seen as fusing into a middle mass. The Westleys[10] have described these 'emerging workers' as comprising a broad central stratum enjoying a common, mass-consumption style of life within which there are quantitative differences but no sharp qualitative contrasts. Some families within this middle mass are able to afford more expensive furnishings and holidays than others, but being unrelated to other inequalities, such differences are not liable to result in perceptions of the families concerned belonging to different classes with opposing interests.

In socialist countries the 'official' belief system argues a trend towards incongruence. Socialist regimes claim that their societies are classless, not that social equality has arrived. Inequalities are justified in terms of a need for incentives which reward individuals for exceptional contributions.[11] It is claimed, however, that inequalities of income, occupational prestige, housing and educational opportunity are becoming dissociated with the result that non-antagonistic strata replace classes with conflicting interests.[12] Socialist writers assert that these trends are only possible alongside socialist relations of production, but some western sociologists claim comparable developments in capitalist societies. According to their arguments, manual work might be retaining much of its traditional character, but this type of employment is losing its association with other inequalities thereby blurring the old middle working class schism.

An opposing school of thought rejects the multi-dimensional view and argues that stratification is fundamentally uni-dimensional. Other inequalities are regarded as derived from one basic underlying class division. Orthodox Marxists argue that capitalist relations of production necessarily generate inequalities of income and wealth, from which differences in power, educational opportunity and life-style follow. In the short term, the scope for autonomous action in the superstructure may obscure fundamental class divisions, but in the longer term this view predicts a growing consistency, congruence or crystallization amongst different types of inequality leading to the polarization of classes that will then recognize their antagonistic interests.

The embourgeoisement thesis is the best-known example of the 'emergent incongruence' viewpoint, the term embourgeoisement referring to a process whereby manual workers and their families are drawn up and assimilated into the middle classes. Some writers claim embourgeoisement as an accelerating trend, and to do their arguments justice it is necessary to recognize that no sociologists have been so simple-minded as to claim that affluence alone is sufficient to have this effect. What is argued is that rising income levels in concert with other changes including the redistribution of educational opportunities, the spread of home ownership and the marketing for mass consumption of material and cultural elements in former middle class life-styles are progressively blurring the traditional middle- working class cleavage. Embourgeoisement inevitably changes the middle class which not only grows in size but has its baseline lowered to a point within rather than above the manual strata, changing the overall shape of the class structure from a pyramid with a numerically dominant working class at the base to a diamond in which a middle mass is the major element.

In Britain Millar[13] claims such an overall trend, in the 1950s Zweig's research amongst workers in 'advanced' sectors of the economy including the electrical goods industry envisaged an erosion of the working class,[14] whilst Turner's subsequent research amongst the well-paid car makers of the 1960s indicated similar developments.[15] Turner portrayed car workers as uprooted from traditional working class communities, enjoying high earnings upon which they built individualized, home-centred life-styles incorporating middle class tastes including holidays abroad and dining out. These workers appeared part-way towards adopting middle class values such as desiring educational success for their children, whilst working class identities and Labour Party loyalties were judged nominal and wavering. Subsequent pieces of evidence have lent further support to the embourgeoisement thesis. For example, Butler and Stokes' surveys of political attitudes and behaviour have revealed that within the manual strata, relatively high earnings and home ownership are related to workers describing themselves as 'middle class'.[16] Ineichen's research amongst wives on three private and one council estate has shown that, amongst manual families, even if not synonymous with assimilation into the middle class, home ownership is related to a movement towards middle class life-styles.[17]

Forecasts of embourgeoisement are sometimes linked with the observation that the proportion of manual jobs in the labour force is falling, thereby dramatizing the impending decline of the working class. In 1911 only 25 per cent of all jobs were in the white-collar sector, whereas by 1961 it was 38 per cent, and by 1971 43 per cent. This trend is due to an industry-effect and an occupation-effect. Industrialization involves, in the first instance, a movement of labour from primary activities (farming, fishing and mining) into the secondary manufacturing sector. Subsequently labour moves into 'tertiary', service industries such as banking, insurance, health and education. Advanced economies generate a growing demand for services in which the labour force is mainly white-collar. The occupation-effect occurs within industries and results from the concentration of activity in large corporations together with scientific and technological progress. New occupations are created for executives, scientists, technologists, administrators and clerks. As a result of these trends it is envisaged that in Britain by the end of the century there will be more white-collar than manual workers. In the USA blue-collar workers are already a minority group. The manual labour force is ceasing to comprise the mass of the people. Couple these scenarios of fewer manual workers and the more advanced sections of those remaining being assimilated into a middle mass, and the future working class stands portrayed as a declining force.

The internal stratification of the working class

The incongruence viewpoint has a companion theory which argues that clearer divisions are appearing within a formerly more homogeneous manual workforce. This theory about the internal stratification of the working class has won most favour amongst American sociologists. Following a comparative study of automobile workers in the USA, Italy, Argentina and India, W. H. Form has concluded that as industrial development progresses, the skilled strata become increasingly differentiated from other manual workers.[18] This differentiation is not merely in terms of income. Equally important, Form noted a tendency to participate, far less evident amongst other manual workers, both in work-related and other social organizations extending beyond family and neighbourhood communities. As a result of their propensity to participate, skilled workers were the most effective trade unionists, securing not only high earnings but other fringe benefits. Political activists tended to be drawn from this stratum, whose members were also exceptionally sensitive to the implications of education for future life-chances. Form found that the contrast between skilled and other manual workers was particularly marked in the more advanced industrial societies. He argues, therefore, that rather than homogenizing and polarizing the working class, the development of industrialism progressively splinters the manual strata, and the prospects of a radical, unified labour movement recede.

Mackenzie has drawn comparable conclusions from his study of craftsmen and other workers on Rhode Island.[19] He argues, like Form, that with the evolution of industrialism the class structure becomes more rather than less complex. Of particular relevance to this discussion, Mackenzie's evidence suggests that a skilled and well-paid stratum of manual workers is differentiated from the remainder of the working class. In terms of life-styles and political allegiances, Mackenzie's craftsmen remained distinguishable from the lowest grade of white-collar workers that he examined. Hence his reservations about the embourgeoisement thesis. At the same time, 70 per cent of the craftsmen defined themselves as middle class and the group as a whole displayed strong 'bourgeois' aspirations in the sense of desiring promotion for themselves and educational success for their children.

Arguments about the internal differentiation of the working class can be linked with economists' observations, again mainly in America, about the creation of a 'dual labour market'.[20] Rather than conceiving the entire work-force as participating in a single labour market, this theory insists that it is more realistic to think in terms of a series of segmented markets between which there is little mobility. Within the manual work-force, there is a primary market composed of relatively skilled, well-paid and strongly unionized workers, who have access to the more secure jobs in larger companies and other concerns that can offer attractive conditions of employment. On the other side of the dual labour market workers are non-skilled, only weakly or non-unionized and low paid. Their jobs are relatively insecure, mainly in the smaller firms whose existence is threatened by any down-turn in the trade cycle. Movement into the primary labour market is difficult, access to jobs and training opportunities being restricted by the unions. In addition, in the secondary market employees acquire irregular work habits which reduce their attractiveness to employers. Dual labour market theorists explain the disadvantages of ethnic minorities, women and other groups subject to discrimination in terms of their exclusion from the primary sector. An implication of this argument is that trade unions do not further the interests of the working class as a whole, but rather concentrate advantages within privileged sections at the expense of low wages and intermittant employment elsewhere. Economists who have examined the long-term effects of trade unions and collective bargaining in Britain have concluded that the unions can move their own members up the 'league table' at the expense of other workers, and that they can provoke an overall increase in money wages, but that the real wages of the entire labour force can only be redistributed, not enlarged, by trade unionism.[21] The lower working class that is confined in the secondary labour market, as distinguished by this theory, cannot be likened to a lumpenproletariat or reserve army, the difference being the absence of mobility into 'regular' employment. The more privileged manual strata are not threatened or held in check by would-be competitors. Rather do their privileges depend upon the maintenance of the division between the upper and lower levels of the manual labour force.

This internal stratification theory can be treated as an alternative or complementary to arguments about the growth of incongruence and embourgeoisement. Mackenzie argues that the working class is becoming increasingly divided without its upper layers fusing with the white-collar strata to form a middle mass, the net result being a more complex class structure than formerly with a greater number of divisions. When the internal stratification of the working class is seen as accompanying a fusion of its upper layers into a middle mass, a cleavage cutting through the manual strata is identified as replacing the traditional working- middle class division as the major split in the class structure. On either interpretation, when set alongside the declining proportion of all jobs in the manual sector, the overall conclusion is a decline in the working class both numerically and in the strength that accompanies solidarity.

Goyder's observation of a declining relationship between objective and subjective indicators is consistent with this view of how the class structure is changing.[22] After scrutinising surveys conducted at various points since the Second World War, Goyder has detected in America, and also in Britain though here the evidence is less substantial, a gradual weakening of the relationship between individuals' 'objective' class positions, usually measured by their occupations, and their subjective class identities. Manual workers are increasingly describing themselves as middle class, whilst white-collar employees have become more likely to identify with the working class. These are the trends that incongruence theory leads us to anticipate. Dennis Wrong's argument about a movement towards 'inequality without stratification' is another way of summarizing the anticipated effects of growing incongruence.[23] The functionalist theory implies that inequalities should tend towards this form, with different positions and actors being rewarded in proportion to the value of their contributions to society as a whole. The official ideologies in socialist societies offer such a functionalist interpretation of their own inequalities, and argue that the trend is away from potentially antagonistic divisions. Likewise theories which postulate a splintering of the working class and the emergence of a middle mass in western societies, are suggesting that the inequalities which persist within the working population are ceasing to fall into a pattern that is liable to generate conflict and perceptions of divergent interests.

Embourgeoisement or a new working class?

Since the mid-1960s, British sociology has been almost unanimously critical of the view that advanced sections of the blue-collar strata are merging into a middle mass. The embourgeoisement thesis enjoyed its greatest popularity in the post-1959 period, when the Labour Party had lost three consecutive general elections, by wider margins on each occasion. The theory not only explained the Conservative Party's popularity, but harmonized with other trends. The early 1960s was the age when we had 'never had it so good'; commentators were impressed by the consumer affluence that had arisen as a result of full employment combined with sustained, if modest, economic growth. It was an age of 'growthmanship'. Economists and politicians alike expressed confidence that economic growth would continue, and debated only whose policies would achieve the faster growth rates. The dawning era appeared characterized by an end of ideology and the dominance of consensus politics. Socialism and capitalism began to look less like juxtaposed utopias, and more like alternative means of progressing towards an agreed end – yet greater prosperity for all. Since 1964 the Labour Party has established a claim to the title of 'normal governing party'. Doubts have arisen as to whether economic growth can be permanently sustained, and whether it improves the quality of life in any case. Life in the affluent society has turned somewhat sour. With governments struggling to control wage levels, inflation and the balance of payments, industrial conflict has periodically intensified, and sociological analysis has mirrored these trends, concentrating on sources of class conflict rather than embourgeoisement.

The Affluent Worker is the best-known example of the literature to follow this changing mood.[24] The study was based on interviews with 229 manual workers from three Luton firms, and 54 white-collar employees who were studied for comparative purposes. The findings are relevant to a number of issues concerning the state of the working class, and the study will feature in following chapters, but a principal aim was to appraise the embourgeoisement thesis. The manual workers were all aged between twenty-one and forty-six and therefore had no personal experience of pre-war economic conditions, and all enjoyed earnings above the national average. Industry in Luton was typically modern and capital intensive rather than traditional and declining. In all these respects the investigators could claim their sample as 'prototypical'. If embourgeoisement was occurring anywhere, they argued that it would be evident in Luton. Their findings, however, failed to support the embourgeoisement thesis. *The Affluent Worker* suggests a need to distinguish between the economic, relational and normative dimensions of embourgeoisement. The manual workers in Luton were bourgeois in certain strictly economic terms. Earnings were equal to salary levels in many white-collar jobs, and life-styles offered plentiful evidence of this. For example, 59 per cent were buying their own houses. However, whilst comparable incomes *may* lead to social assimilation and the adoption of middle class values, they need not *necessarily* do so. In Luton the manual sample remained separate from the middle classes in terms of social relationships. They had few white collar friends. Indeed, although they were often migrants from other parts of Britain who had been attracted to Luton by the high wages available and were not immersed in long-settled working class communities, kin and neighbours remained the mainstays of social life outside the workplace. Wider circles of friends and associational ties were more prominent amongst the middle class sample. Rather than being bourgeois, the Luton workers' life-styles seemed better described as privatized. Traditional working class social networks based on kin and neighbours had been diluted, without being replaced by characteristically middle class life-styles. Similarly the values of the Luton workers remained far from bourgeois. Only 12 per cent had voted Conservative at the previous general election and 71 per cent had voted Labour, actually outstripping the national level of Labour support amongst the manual strata.

Why did middle class wage levels fail to provoke a generalized process of embourgeoisement? The Luton investigators saw the answer in so many of their sample's circumstances, particularly at work, remaining distinctly working class. Work, even when well paid, continued to be experienced as labour. The Luton workers were conscious of having to 'earn' their money. Affluence was purchased by accepting shift work and such overtime as available. They did not experience the intrinsic satisfactions that the middle classes more frequently find and had little prospect of promotion. The Luton enquiry suggests that whilst these features of blue-collar life persist, distinctly working class values will continue to appeal irrespective of events outside the workplace.[25]

Other studies have endorsed this conclusion; that rising wage levels and affluent life-styles are insufficient to dissolve working class attitudes and loyalties. Cannon's[26] enquiry amongst 100 compositors in twenty-eight London firms revealed a highly paid group of manual workers who were able to afford many commodities including houses, cars and telephones that have been considered characteristic of middle class life-styles. Yet 77 per cent identified themselves as working class and 68 per cent voted Labour. Apart from providing the compositors with decent incomes, their occupation encouraged continuous interaction with colleagues, consolidated by the trade union chapel, frequent outings and pass-rounds. The result was a strong occupational community which conserved working class sentiments.

No one denies that some manual workers do identify with the middle class and vote Conservative. The association between manual employment and working class values has never been more than a powerful tendency. However, arguments about embourgeoisement and the emergence of a middle mass go beyond noting 'deviant' cases to suggest that they are becoming more numerous, and it is this allegation that critics challenge. As a result of the research that the theory has stimulated we have become more knowledgeable about the circumstances that do encourage manual workers to adopt bourgeois identities, and scepticism of embourgeoisement as an accelerating trend has risen accordingly. The manual strata's working class identities are likely to be relinquished only when rising wage levels are accompanied by a syndrome of other developments.[27] Bourgeois outcomes become probable when manual workers enjoy not only middle class incomes, but possess kinship ties with the middle classes, live in owner-occupied and predominantly middle class districts, are only weakly involved in work-based social relationships and are educated beyond the norm for future manual workers. This *configuration* of circumstances remains rare, and is as likely to be self-arresting as accelerating, for some of the conditions that encourage bourgeois outcomes can only be experienced by atypical groups. Enjoying *relatively* high incomes may encourage manual workers whose circumstances are otherwise favourable to identify with the middle classes, but once achieved by the majority the incomes in question cease encouraging recipients to feel above the working class. Similarly if the majority of manual workers became home owners, this status would lose its bourgeois connotations.

Faced with evidence of the impediments, amongst British sociologists the debate as to whether advanced sectors of the manual strata are fusing into a middle mass has subsided, to be replaced by discussion as to whether a 'new' working class is replacing more traditional varieties. *The Affluent Worker* enquiry pointed to the emergence of a privatized working class, integrated into neither neighbourhood nor workplace communities, and supporting trade unions and the Labour Party for pragmatic rather than traditional solidaristic reasons. The researchers in Luton saw close parallels between the work and non-work situations of their prototypical sample. Semi-skilled process work in modern capital-intensive plants did not foster the solidaristic work–group relationships considered characteristic of traditional crafts and industries. Orientations towards work, therefore, were almost purely instrumental. Work was regarded simply as a means of earning money. There was no evidence of the involvement in work characteristic of middle class occupations. The Luton workers did not identify with their firms or become integrated in social relationships with managerial personnel. Rather than seeking personal mobility they recognized that future prospects depended upon collective action and therefore remained attached to trade unions and the Labour Party, but for instrumental rather than solidaristic motives. The investigators discovered that the Luton workers mostly regarded themselves as belonging not to a bottom working class, but to a large centrally-positioned layer in the social system. Positions within this central stratum were seen as depending upon purchasing power; hence the phrase 'pecuniary imagery' that the investigators coined to described the outlooks of these 'commodity conscious' workers. Whilst the *researchers* argued that the Luton sample remained unassimilated into the middle class, many of their *respondents* did regard themselves as part of a middle mass straddling the traditional blue- white-collar cleavage.

This proposition about a new working class differs from American arguments about internal stratification. The Luton team's new working class is not conceived as an aristocracy of labour. The distinction between the old and the new is lateral rather than vertical. The argument is that over time more traditional forms of working class community and consciousness are being superseded, rather than that the manual strata are being subdivided into superimposed layers.

Critics of *The Affluent Worker* have disputed whether traditional loyalties and solidarity are really being eroded. The Luton team stress the prototypical character of their sample, but doubts have arisen as to whether circumstances in Luton will become increasingly typical. In his study of the relocation of the Birds factory from Birmingham to Banbury, Michael Mann found that the workers were more 'employment dependent' than the Luton sample.[28] The Birds workers enjoyed high earnings which they valued, and could have been labelled instrumentally-oriented, but in addition they valued their security of employment, the seniority and entitlement to fringe benefits that many had accumulated. There is some point in Mann's rhetorical question as to why his, rather than the Luton sample, should not be considered prototypical.

Research in other industries has uncovered trends towards rather than away from allegedly traditional forms of proletarian solidarity. Chivers' study amongst 629 chefs and cooks in London and the West Midlands discusses how employment in these trades has switched from household catering towards restaurants and hotels where conditions are more conducive to solidaristic relationships and sentiments.[29] Although only a minority of those interviewed had already become trade unionists, Chivers found widespread support for trade union representation amongst his sample. Similarly, following their study of shipbuilding workers in Wallsend, Brown and his colleagues describe the weakening of traditional divisions between crafts and company mergers as favouring the development of a generalized class awareness and solidarity.[30] Davis and Cousins, who were involved in this Wallsend enquiry, have argued that the Luton sample should definitely not be regarded as representative of any new working class.[31] Ever since the industrial revolution, they argue, new industries have been attracting migrant labour to expanding towns. The Durham pit villages, as described by Robert Moore,[32] were such 'mini-Lutons' in the nineteenth century, attracting workers who were presumably instrumentally-oriented, seeking the big money. In such circumstances both workplace and community life must be initially privatized, but time alone may be sufficient for solidaristic attachments to evolve. Other commentators have argued that if workplace and neighbourhood solidarity really is declining, this could promote rather than undermine more general working class loyalties. According to this view, local attachments obstruct workers' perceptions of society-wide class divisions. Hence the withering of these attachments and the consequent exposure of the cash nexus as the worker's basic relationship to the means of production could supply the conditions for an escalation of genuine class consciousness. Robin Blackburn offers such a prediction, pointing out that objective inequalities between manual workers and more privileged strata have not narrowed.[33] Indeed, Blackburn argues, in some respects the situation of the blue-collar worker has become more exploited with capital-intensive methods leading to a spread of shift work and pressure to maximize output, often despite risks of injury and unhealthy conditions.

From the uncertainty surrounding the arguments the one firm conclusion we can draw is that the net pattern of historical change is more likely to be subtle than dramatic. It is unwise to mistake temporary or localized trends for the longer-term historical tide, and some trends that have excited considerable comment have been confined to limited sections of the manual labour force. In some industries such as motor vehicle assembly, technological changes have militated against solidaristic workgroups and left workers privatized along monotonous assembly lines. But elsewhere, as in the service trades described by Chivers, the major organizational and technological trends have contrary implications. In some districts urban redevelopment has been destroying working class communities and rehousing privatized families, but many of the earlier settled council estates are now Labour strongholds harbouring numerous working class organizations. The final verdict on the net result of these trends must await future history and subsequent analysis, but it seems improbable that the contemporary working class stands on the verge of any major transformation; towards privatization, revolutionary class consciousness or embourgeoisement.

Some American commentators suspect that British sociologists are dispensing with the middle mass theory too hastily. For example, the Westleys[34] together with Katona and his colleagues[35] have argued that western Europe in general and Britain in particular lag behind America in socio-economic development, and are still hampered by the depth and rigidity of traditional class divisions. Given time and a reacceleration of economic growth, their arguments suggest that Britain's manual workers will begin to fuse into a middle mass. We must continue to recognize this possibility. Simultaneously, we must also heed those American sociologists who have begun to express doubts as to the alleged decline of the working class in the USA. For instance, Levison argues that the majority of Americans remain distinctly working class.[36] Amongst males, if individuals in routine clerical and service jobs are included, 60 per cent of all American workers are in manual occupations and, compared with others, these workers continue to receive relatively low pay. Furthermore, according to Levison's evidence, rather than being assimilated into classless suburbs, blue-collar families in America congregate in cheaper housing districts. Patricia and Brendan Sexton have also attacked the view that American blue-collar workers enjoy a middle class status and income.[37] According to the Sextons, this is just one amongst many myths that result in the predicament of the working class being overlooked. Politicians along with pressure groups campaign for the poor and ethnic minorities, whilst the American blue-collar worker is considered able to bear the cost of the resultant welfare measures. The Sextons attribute blue-collar America's 'hard hat' conservative attitudes towards 'welfare' and 'the poor', to its own problems being neglected by intellectuals and politicians.

Decomposition, homogenization and British working class

It is far from easy to apply arguments about the internal stratification of the working class to British trends. The relevance of this (originally American) theory in Britain is far from self-evident.[38] There have always been differences of income, status and job security amongst manual workers. But are these differences becoming increasingly wide or deepening with clearer divisions of interest and life-style as the internal stratification theory suggests?

In Britain the income differentials between skilled and non-skilled manual workers have been narrowing rather than widening.[39] In the nineteenth century an aristocracy of labour with skill in its hands could be easily distinguished from workers who had nothing but labour, crude muscle power, to sell. Admission to skilled trades was controlled by apprenticeships leading to jobs that were not only better paid but usually more secure than other grades of employment, and therefore provided the basis for 'respectable' life-styles. Subsequently not only have pay differentials been compressed but the jobs have become more alike. Technological change has transferred skill from craftsmen's hands into machines, and has simultaneously taken the muscle power out of labouring. Hence the trend towards all manual workers becoming operatives of machinery, admittedly of differing degrees of complexity. In the second half of the nineteenth century the modern trade unions appeared, at first confined to skilled trades, but the movement subsequently spread to cover all types of manual employment. There is more evidence of homogenization than decomposition within Britain's manual work-force.

Another trend running contrary to the internal stratification theory concerns the treatment of categories of workers formerly excluded from the more attractive occupations. School-leavers who failed to secure apprenticeships were once sentenced to casual and dead-end jobs, whilst women and racial minorities have been concentrated in non-skilled, lower-paid employment. The overall trends have been towards easing the disadvantages of these groups. School-leavers have benefited from the expansion of education and training opportunities which, alongside the full employment that prevailed from 1945 to the early 1970s, forced casual and dead-end jobs off the market and closed the gap between adolescent and adult rates of pay. Legislation has outlawed job discrimination on racial and sexual grounds, and equal pay for women has become a statutory requirement. Neither women nor blacks are yet fully assimilated throughout the labour force, but any trend is in this direction.

If the internal stratification theory has any validity in Britain it can only be in relation to a 'new claiming class'. Until the Second World War poverty was a common working class condition. The surveys of Booth, Rowntree and others had revealed that at any time around a third of all working class families were living beneath or barely above the poverty line, meaning that their incomes were insufficient to purchase the necessities of life. In addition to charting its prevalence, these surveys revealed that poverty was not confined to the exceptionally indolent. Rather was poverty a condition to which the entire working class was at risk at certain points in the life-cycle, particularly the child-rearing phase and old age, and in the event of misfortunes such as unemployment and chronic ill-health which individuals could do little to prevent. The poor were not a separate stratum, nor was poverty a risk to which only a lower working class was exposed. Poverty was a working class problem. During the 1950s it became widely believed that poverty was eradicated. The prevailing belief was that full employment and the welfare state had lifted everyone above the poverty line. Subsequently this belief was shattered. Poverty was rediscovered within the affluent society. This rediscovery involved a subtle redefinition of the concept. It was argued that, rather than an absolute level supposedly valid in all times and places, poverty should be defined in relative terms; that conceptions of a tolerable minimum should be related to prevailing norms and standards of propriety. The wisdom of this redefinition is not crucial to the current discussion. It is sufficient to note that the information collected by, amongst others, Townsend and Abel-Smith,[40] revealed that the poor were lagging as far behind the average as ever, and that the numbers in the tail of the economic procession were tending to increase rather than decline. Two sections of the population were especially liable to fall into this tail. Firstly, families entirely dependent upon state benefits, amongst whom retirement pensioners were the most numerous. Secondly, large families dependent upon a single low wage-earner, though in this equation 'large' might involve no more than three or even two children, whilst a 'low' wage could mean only slightly beneath the average. Poverty not only persisted, but its location seemed to have changed little since the 1930s.

According to one argument, subsequent developments, some of which were intended to ameliorate the conditions of the above groups, have unintentionally created a new claiming class. Firstly, the unemployment rate has risen to a level not envisaged in the 1960s. By 1977 approximately one-and-a-half million individuals, roughly 6 per cent of the labour force, were registered as unemployed. In the late 1950s half a million out of work was considered an unacceptable level of unemployment. The higher level now prevailing means that greater numbers of those who could be economically active are pushed into the ranks of the poor. Secondly, the failure of governments to raise income tax thresholds in line with the rate of inflation has created a fiscal drag which makes workers on below-average wages, and sometimes even those with earnings beneath the minimum level prescribed by the Supplementary Benefits Commission, liable to tax. Thirdly, since the late 1960s a series of means-tested benefits have been introduced including rent and rate rebates and the Family Income Supplement, the object being to target financial assistance towards those in greatest need. One effect has been the 'poverty trap'. The larger number of households whose members now suffer unemployment or the companion condition, intermittent employment, along with other dependents on state benefits, find it virtually impossible to improve their standards of living. Increases in earnings can be completely wiped out by loss of means-tested benefits and income tax.

Jordan[41] has talked of a 'new Speenhamland system' creating a new claiming class - paupers whose prospects depend upon their effectiveness as claimants, and who are therefore liable to be labelled 'scroungers' by other members of the public. In Jordan's view social policy has trapped a section of the population within this claiming class which, he alleges, is becoming increasingly distinguishable from the independent working class. Means-tested benefits coupled with the principle of 'less eligibility' – insisting that recipients of benefits accept inferior standards of living to what they could secure from earned income – imprison a section of the population at the minimum level that the state considers tolerable. Other analysts of the 'cycle of deprivation' argue that families become locked in poverty as a result of socially transmitted inadequacies. Inadequate parents fail to improve their own circumstances, and fail to develop in their children the qualities required for self-improvement. Sir Keith Joseph has been a persistent advocate of policies designed to break this poverty cycle.[42] According to Jordan, it is social policy rather than inadequacies in the individuals affected that keeps the poverty cycle locked. Despite disagreement as to the nature of the imprisoning forces, however, both argue that a claiming stratum has become distinguishable from the main body of the working class.

Following a study in St Ann's, a deprived district in Nottingham, Coates and Silburn have offered a lucid description of the culture of poverty.[43] In St Ann's 37 per cent of the population's incomes fell below a line 40 per cent above the supplementary benefit level, which has become a conventional 'rule-of-thumb' measure of poverty. Information from interviews in the district illustrates the atmosphere of fatalism and hopelessness that develops when families have no prospect of raising themselves to what would ordinarily be considered a decent standard of living. This is how poverty can become a self-sustaining condition.

Arguments about exactly how the poverty trap is kept in place – through inadequacies transmitted in the family or by social policy – can be left unresolved in the present discussion. Similarly we need not weigh the merits of the various proposals for enabling the poor to break through the trap. Jordan advocates a guaranteed minimum income, pitched much closer to the average than current welfare levels. Joseph seeks more effective means of intervening selectively so as to make an impact where the need is greatest. Rhodes Boyson proposes to abolish the poor by *reducing* welfare expenditure as a practical lesson in the virtues of self-reliance.[44] The point that all these analyses share in common is a view of the poor as a separate stratum from the working class with little mobility between these strata.

A different view is implicit in Margaret Wynn's analysis of *Family Policy*.[45] Wynn argues that during the 1960s state benefits to families with dependent children, such as family allowances, failed to rise at an equal pace with other incomes, and nowhere near met the cost of children to a household. As a result, Wynn argues, the relative economic standing of families with dependent children deteriorated, accentuating the cyclical incidence of poverty that has been evident since the nineteenth century, with working class households experiencing a plunge in their standards of living during the child-rearing phase. Likewise Kincaid's comprehensive analysis of social security in Britain identifies poverty as a general working class problem.[46] Kincaid shows that the tax and welfare systems involve little net redistribution from rich to poor, and that overall economic inequality in Britain has hardly declined since 1945. In practice the social security system transfers income within the working class; from wage earners to individuals at points in the life-cycle when they are economically inactive such as old age, and to those who suffer misfortunes such as serious ill-health and unemployment. Compared with the wealthy, the entire working class remains impoverished, and at vulnerable points in the life-cycle families are at risk of their living standards plunging to the modest minimum considered tolerable by the state. This analysis treats the poor and the working class, if not synonymous, as overlapping groups. The poor are conceived not as a residual stratum but simply as the working class at particularly vulnerable phases.

Rutter and Madge[47] have attempted a systematic appraisal of the theory that poverty has become a socially transmitted condition, and Analysing all the available data about numerous types of deprivation, Analysing all the available data about numerous tyupes of deprivation, they assess the continuities that persist over time and between generations. Their conclusion, that the discontinuities are more numerous than the continuities casts doubt upon the cyclical and underclass theories. Continuities are more frequent than would be expected by chance, and there is evidence, presented by other authors, of a poverty trap. On balance, however, the evidence requires caution before we conclude that the barrier above the poor has become sufficiently severe to justify treating a schism beneath an independent working class as of comparable significance to the cleavage between the working class and superordinate strata.

The persistence of the working class

The evidence in this and the preceding chapter unequivocally points to the persistence of the British working class. Talk of 'one nation' is as much wishful thinking today as in Disraeli's era. Manual occupations are not losing their working class character. Furthermore, changes outside the workplace principally resulting from higher standards of living are not leading manual employees *en mass* to abandon their working class identities. The accumulation of research now enables us to dismiss ideas about economic and technological progress irresistibly merging blue-collar workers into a middle mass. In addition, despite the inequalities and other differences that exist within the manual strata, their similar experiences of work continue to encourage a common identification with the working class, trade union membership and support for the Labour Party. As yet the organizations and types of action that working class culture supports have neither transformed the status of the manual worker nor overturned differentials. Pay rises and the development of the social services have done little more than maintain the relative position of the working class. Despite impressions to the contrary, the working class has been running hard in order to stand still, and its victories have mostly been defensive rather than offensive.

Evidence regarding trends over time is always difficult to assess, but the more systematic investigations are virtually unanimous in rejecting forecasts of a middle mass obliterating the middle–working class schism. The live arguments concern whether the working class is changing *without* merging with the middle classes. Does the contemporary working class differ from its predecessors? Similarly, whilst there is debate as to whether a new claiming class is appearing, there are no signs of divisions within or beneath the manual strata as clear as the break above the working class. Amongst manual workers in employment, no deepening divisions of interest or circumstance are apparent. Britain's class structure is not changing towards a closer resemblance with the functionalist model. Whatever this theory maintains, Britain's class structure continues to look most unlike either a sliding scale or a large number of small steps with no major schisms. Whether or not some system of stratification is functionally inevitable, the functionalist model does not bear a helpful resemblance to the British class structure. It is because the working class lives on, that terms like manual and blue-collar continue to be meaningful amongst the public. As acknowledged previously, the boundary above the working class is blurred. No one pretends that the division between the working class and other strata is crystal clear, yet it remains a real and persistent cleavage. When they analyse this division, sociologists are not discovering a fact of life about which members of the public are otherwise unaware. Sociology has not invented the class structure. The subject only makes explicit a division in the social hierarchy that people acknowledge and encounter in everyday life.

Whether the Marxist theory fits reality more closely than the functionalist model is a question that, for the present, can be left in abeyance. The evidence surveyed so far is not inconsistent with the view that the manual section of the proletariat is part way towards becoming fully class conscious as a result of the deprivations that capitalism inflicts. At the same time, the evidence discussed has not proved that stratification is basically uni-dimensional with all inequalities tending towards a similar pattern that will eventually polarize the working class. What has been demonstrated is that even if and when their life-styles outside the workplace share features in common with the middle classes, this is insufficient to result in blue-collar employees' working class identities, together with their trade union and Labour Party loyalties, being abandoned.

Family, community and life-styles 4

When analysing the class structure the family deserves more than cursory attention. The family's role includes the procreation and socialization of children who, therefore, do not all enter society on the same footing. They are born into particular families in different social classes and this gives the class structure a persistence from generation to generation. Education and other channels through which social mobility can occur allow some individuals to change their class positions, but as we shall see in the next chapter, few move far from the levels where they are born. This is because, despite some claims to the contrary, family life and the treatment of children are not 'just the same' irrespective of social class. Its members' positions in the social hierarchy have implications for the character of family life whose net effect is to reproduce the class structure – to nurture children for adulthoods in the social classes into which they are initially born.

The passing of the traditional working class community

During the 1950s sociology 'discovered' the traditional working class community. Previously urbanization had been linked with the community's demise. The anonymity of cities was contrasted against the personalized relationships of rural society. Genuine communities were known to persist in industrial villages, including the pit villages,[1] but this traditional way of life was considered incompatible with the city. The demise of community was coupled with an alleged decline of the family. Industrialization was seen as stripping the family of former functions including economic production, education and the care of dependents which became responsibilities of the welfare state. The declining birth rate, married women working and rising divorce figures were all taken as indicative of weakening family relationships. Kinship was regarded as having lost its former importance, leaving isolated nuclear units lacking the stability associated with multi-functional families.

During the 1950s a developing and empirically based British sociology, in which the *Institute of Community Studies* founded in London's East End was influential, discovered urban villages in the heart of Britain's cities.[2] Calling these communities 'traditional' was never intended to mean that they necessarily belonged to the past but that, as in rural social relationships, time and tradition were important factors in their sustenance. Following the early traumas of industrialism and urbanization, working class districts had acquired settled populations that were born, grew up and continued to live in their localities. The inhabitants typically found employment in local industries such as the East End's docks into which son followed father. Housing was mainly privately rented, and acquired by established tenants 'speaking for' their children, as fathers spoke for sons at work. Within such milieux a sense of community is virtually inescapable. Residents feel a consciousness of kind. They share an awareness of facing common problems and mix with an effortless sociability. Neighbourliness becomes natural and is continuously cemented in pubs, streets, corner shops, workplaces and homes. Formal associations including darts leagues, brass bands, Sunday schools and working men's clubs in addition to trade unions and the Labour Party have been rooted in these traditional and solidaristic communities.[3] Some texts give a rosy, romanticized view of traditional working class life, neglecting that family feuds as well as friendships often cut deeply, and forgetting the grinding hardship that helped to thrust neighbours into mutual dependence. Nevertheless, the point holds that physically dilapidated slum areas have been socially rich.

Alongside the working class community, the sociology of the 1950s also rediscovered the extended family. In traditional working class areas it had reappeared as a virile institution. Sex roles tended to be segregated. Men's social lives were spent with mates in pubs and clubs. Home and family were women's territory. But this lack of conjugal togetherness was shown not to indicate any weakness in family life. Extended kinship systems were held together principally through female lineages. Mothers surrounded by grown up and married daughters laid the framework for family life. The working class extended family has been appropriately called a women's trade union. In traditional working class communities female relatives have ordinarily seen each other daily. Men are peripheral to the main trunk of family life. Married couples normally obtain housing close to the wife's parents, often as a result of the wife's mother speaking to the landlord. Working class parents know that 'A son's a son till he gets a wife, a daughter's a daughter all her life'. For all its members the working class extended family has acted as a constant source of advice and sociability. It has supplied relatives who are always available to assist in times of need including old age,[4] during the child-rearing phase, in times of unemployment and sickness. In traditional working class communities, inter-locking kinship systems have given residents intricate networks of uncles, cousins and aunts, helping to knit neighbourhoods into cohesive units.

Having discovered traditional working class communities and families sociology immediately began to chart their demise. In this tale of destruction, local authority planning and housing departments featured as the principal villains. Following the Second World War, local authorities recommenced their housing programmes which involved tearing traditional slum areas apart and resettling not whole communities or even extended families, but nuclear households. Sociology discovered the traditional working class community before policy-makers and implementers became aware of its importance. In the brave new world after 1945, a prime objective of social policy was to rehouse families from slums – to provide more spacious, healthier and brighter accommodation. The middle classes had led the drift to the suburbs, and local authorities were equipped with the planning powers and finance to enable the working class to follow suit. The intentions were laudable. Before the 1960s few questioned the desirability of slum clearance. Some working class families had understandable reservations about leaving well-known districts and homes, but the majority welcomed the prospect of a bright new suburban life, with space and opportunities for the kids of which their grandparents had only been able to dream.[5] Sociologists quickly began to show how the suburban dream was turning sour. Studies of suburban council estates found that families certainly appreciated their gardens, bathrooms and other mod cons. At the same time, they often complained about the higher rents and the expense of furnishing their new homes, and of how financial pressures were aggravated by longer journeys to work. More lamentably, many felt that although materially improved, their life-styles had been socially impoverished. They missed the warmth and neighbourliness of their old areas. Women particularly missed the day-to-day contact with kinfolk. Nuclear families were left isolated, distanced from their kin and surrounded by strangers. The appeal of *Coronation Street* and similar television programmes indicates a continuing nostalgia for a passing, older way of life.

Researchers have subsequently turned vindictively towards the planners. Following his research in Rye Hill, a 'twilight' area in Newcastle-upon-Tyne, J. Gower Davies[6] has accused town planners of allowing their power to replace reason. Davies notes how planners claim a professional competence to comprehend the whole situation, to act in the general interest and on behalf of future citizens. He notes how readily they reject the views of 'merelees' such as owner-occupiers who are only and selfishly concerned with their private interests, and how they similarly dismiss the interventions of 'bumbles' including local councillors who are alleged to lack vision. In Davies' view, the damage still being inflicted upon urban communities will only be arrested when the entire planning process is rephrased to treat the public as customers rather than naive clients.

Will traditional communities eventually re-form in the new areas? Willmott's research on the Dagenham estate suggests that the passage of time enables neighbourliness to be established but without a complete return to the old way of life.[7] New estates have been planned spaciously with houses set apart by gardens, and do not force the constant interaction that was unavoidable in the old back-to-backs. Corner shops and pubs are replaced by centres serving larger populations. Housing is allocated through bureaucratic procedures according to measures of need, making it more difficult for married children to secure accommodation close to their parents than when it was necessary only to speak to the rent-man. Work is less likely to be local since planners segregate factories on industrial estates. In all these respects the new districts fail to lay the foundations from which communities in the older areas developed.

Faced with this evidence, since the 1960s local authorities have been seeking alternatives to wholesale slum clearance and rehousing on sprawling estates. Hilda Jennings has researched one such alternative in the Barton Hill area of Bristol where the local council sought to rebuild the district for resettlement by its original inhabitants thereby preserving an existing community.[8] The attempt failed. During the physical rebuilding of Barton Hill residents had to move to new estates, and as the destruction of the old area proceeded a sense of decay arose and people's pride in their district evaporated. Houses were allowed to deteriorate, empty spaces blighted the district and 'transients' began to move in. The new estates were no panaceas. Residents missed their old friends, relatives, local jobs and services. In the absence of community controls, delinquency increased, and 'housing estate neurosis' became rampant. Nevertheless, when the rebuilding was completed many former residents had no desire to return to Barton Hill. Attachments to the district had been eroded in the period leading up to their departures. Amongst former residents who did return, the old community was not rekindled. Extended family and friendship networks had been fragmented, in the new Barton Hill there was no place for corner shops, local businesses and jobs, and the flats in which some returners were settled did not encourage the casual social intercourse that was possible in the old streets.

Alternative recipes for preserving valued features of traditional working class life-styles have included building 'community', or at least the foundations for its growth, into new housing developments. High-rise flats have fallen from favour as occupants so frequently complain of feeling imprisoned. Instead of vast estates, recent developments have grouped houses into neighbourhoods with definite geographical boundaries, served by their own primary schools and shops. Community centres have been erected and, in some districts, community workers appointed, amidst hopes that they will act as catalysts. Instead of isolating tenants behind lengthy gardens, there has been a trend towards 'town houses' resembling the older terraced properties. So far, however, these initiatives have led to no convincing success stories.

Other proposals have sought to substitute 'participation' for the heartless grinding of planning bureaucracies, but research into the reality of participation has not been encouraging. Dennis' enquiries in Millfield,[9] one of the older districts in Sunderland, describe how impotent local residents can become when faced with a planning bureaucracy. Bureaucrats possess information and ideas that local residents are unable to assimilate. Once plans have begun to unfold it is difficult to programme residents' aspirations into their execution. Dennis labels participation a 'façade'. Although many Millfield residents did not really want to move, the majority did little than voice general opposition to the planners' scheme for redevelopment. As far as changing the plans was concerned, little was achieved.

Other proposals for conserving established communities aim to revitalise rather than destroy twilight areas. Yet even when the aim is to restore rather than destroy, the attentions of planners are liable to generate blight. The uncertainty that accompanies tentative plans for a district makes houses difficult to sell. Landlords and tenants refuse to spend money on property that may have no future. Tenants who are able to do so often move to other districts leaving houses empty. Once these processes have begun, blight descends quickly. This happened in the part of Sunderland that Dennis studied, and in the Rye Hill area of Newcastle that Davies investigated.

J. Seabrook's *City Close-Up*,[10] based upon forty depth interviews with people in Blackburn, yields many insights into working class feelings about the overall patterns of post war change. Seabrook describes how economic change has raised standards of material prosperity, but how the traditional working class culture has fallen apart, leaving families feeling alone and without roots. In Seabrook's account the old and the poor emerge as the most unfortunate victims. They are the least able to build new lives. But the social malaise is more widespread, leading to a search for scapegoats, and in Blackburn, the 'Pakis' have presented themselves as convenient targets.

Have the planners and housing departments been blamed for too much? Rehousing has been a frequent catalyst, but further trends have undermined traditional kin and community bonds even in the remaining long-settled working class areas, and these same trends militate against the evolution of new communities in more recently built suburbs. The decline in the birth rate since the nineteenth century has important implications. Since the Second World War the large family with six or more children has become a rarity even amongst the non-skilled manual strata. Today most adults simply do not possess enough brothers, sisters, cousins, nephews and nieces for the extended family to provide the constant support that was possible in the past. Likewise, having reared only one or two children, ageing persons are less able to rely upon relatives remaining close by. The declining birth rate has been accompanied by a movement of married women into the labour force. Today over a half of all married women are in paid employment outside their homes. Women are less domesticated than formerly; they do not spend lifetimes in and around their own and neighbours' houses in the ways that once helped to knit local communities. Economic and occupational change has also contributed to the decline of community. Employment in once-important industries including coal, textiles and the docks has declined. The transport revolution associated with the spread of car ownership has enabled men to seek employment away from their neighbourhoods. In education working class children have become increasingly likely to attend non-neighbourhood grammar or comprehensive schools. Meanwhile the mass media in general and television in particular have been spreading a common culture throughout the land, eroding formerly distinctive neighbourhood traditions. Although it has been a common catalyst, rehousing has probably only accelerated changes that would otherwise have occurred more gradually.

Rather than romanticizing the past, it can be argued that sociologists should stop talking about decline and concentrate upon identifying the new patterns of family and neighbourhood life that are emerging in response to contemporary conditions. In their study of *The Family and Social Change* in Swansea, Rosser and Harris[11] discuss how the extended family is becoming a looser social network. They explain how the decline in family size, increased rates of social and geographical mobility, the segregation of work and leisure and women's escape from domesticity are transforming kinship into loose and geographically dispersed systems. According to Rosser and Harris, the extended family is not dead. Although it rarely offers the day-to-day support that members were able to expect in traditional communities, it continues to celebrate major events in the life-cycle and provides its members with a sense of identity. The social networks that supply friendship and sociability are ceasing to be concentrated within specific localities. Individuals' networks are now more likely to be geographically scattered and to include a mixture of friends from work, acquaintances struck up during education, past and present neighbours and persons simply met 'socially'. In Rosser and Harris' view, the net pattern of change has led to a convergence between middle and working class styles of family life. Young and Willmott prefer the phrase 'stratified diffusion' but argue similarly that social class contrasts in life-styles are becoming less severe.[12] The theory of stratified diffusion suggests that new styles of life first appear amongst the upper middle classes. Then, as affluence and other opportunities become more widespread, the theory argues that the life-styles of the social vanguard will be increasingly widely emulated. Hence Willmott and Young, describing the symmetrical family in which both domestic and bread-winning tasks are shared out between husband and wife, claim that this type of marriage has become most common amongst the middle classes, but expect it to spread through the manual strata. Eventually, therefore, it is suggested that the symmetrical conjugal unit, surrounded by a loosely extended family and a geographically dispersed network of friends, will become the normal framework for community life at all levels in society.

The Affluent Worker enquiry,[13] which was discussed in the previous chapter, has encouraged doubts as to whether 'advanced' sections of the manual strata are being socially assimilated into the middle classes. The workers interviewed had few middle class friends, compared with the white-collar sample they were less likely to be members of non-workbased associations, and remained more dependent upon family and kin for social intercourse. Yet whilst resisting talk of embourgeoisement and assimilation, the investigators acknowledged a convergence with middle class life-styles, and this is a major issue that examinations of the contemporary working class must confront. With the passing of traditional working class communities, is social class becoming a less effective variable in distinguishing patterns of family and neighbourhood life? Or do manual life-styles remain distinctly working class, albeit in non-traditional ways?

Marriage, home-making and social class

Is the demise of traditional working class communities part of a trend towards classlessness? Some politicians certainly like to stress how the trials and tribulations of family and neighbourhood life give the entire population interests and experiences transcending class boundaries. Some commentators insist that behind the bedroom and drawing room curtains, people's behaviour depends essentially upon their individual characters rather than their social class positions. Sometimes the 'classless youth culture' is hailed as one example of how irrelevant class differences have become. In fact, however, class remains a pervasive influence and continues to penetrate family life. Its consequences today may rarely include the traditional working class community, but they are as discriminating as ever.

Love and marriage are not the same the world over. The processes of selecting marital partners and home-making vary considerably within contemporary Britain depending upon couples' class positions. There may be a generation gap, but young people are not immersed in a classless youth culture. Young people's life-styles present sharp contrasts which are closely related to class origins. When older generations fail to perceive these differences, this only proves how little they understand the young. Compared with adolescents from middle class homes, working class teenagers, especially boys, enjoy the greater freedom from supervision. They 'go out' more often, and spend more time with their peer groups. The majority commence work at sixteen, which adds to their independence. Critics sometimes accuse working class parents of indifference and of abdicating their responsibilities, but within the working class there is a long-established view of adolescence as a 'brief flowering period'.[14] Folk realize that 'You're only young once'. Marriage and parenthood loom and, before they are actually encountered, having a good time is considered entirely sensible. For the working class, youth is a *brief* flowering period. Full-time education usually ends at sixteen, and nowadays girls are mostly married by their early twenties. From before leaving school, marriage is often a conscious female ambition. Work is envisaged as a brief interlude and a secondary concern. This is not altogether unrealistic. For working class girls, job opportunities are usually limited to routine work in shops and factories. Marriage is a way out. It can appear attractive compared with work and, in any case, marriage and motherhood are regarded as natural feminine destinies.[15] Amongst working class boys, from age twelve and sometimes before, leisure is typically centred upon monosexual peer groups. Girls and sex are common topics of conversation, though less frequently objects of action. It is not unusual for working class boys to experience only one serious relationship with a member of the opposite sex. Couples drift into love and marriage is regarded as the inevitable sequel. Grooms tend to be slightly older than their brides, but it is now common for working class males to be embarked on careers as husbands and fathers by their mid-twenties.

Contrast the experience of a working class mother aged twenty, and there are many of them, with a female student of the same age, and it becomes difficult to sustain talk of a classless youth culture. Young people from all social backgrounds may wear different clothes and favour different types of music from their parents, but scratch a little under the surface and the classless façade quickly evaporates. Although it may well sound similar to some elders, young people do not even possess uniform musical tastes, and these variations correspond to social class differences.[16] Young people themselves are well aware of social class. Although many university students extend statements of comradeship towards the working class, they more rarely marry or even mix with them socially. Students have their own sports facilities, societies and parties.

The lives of middle class teenagers are subject to greater adult supervision. As will be explained in the following chapter, they are the more likely to remain in education beyond age sixteen, and therefore lack working class youth's economic independence. Middle class teenagers spend more time at home, and are the more likely to belong to youth clubs.[17] Girls as well as boys frequently display interest in occupational careers and acknowledge a need to postpone marriage and parenthood well beyond their teens.[18] In these senses they achieve adult status the more slowly. In terms of sexual experience, at any given age middle class youth lag behind their working class peers.[19] Students may have acquired a permissive reputation but in practice, on average, they are more celibate than other members of their age group. Amongst his national sample of 16- to 45-year-olds, Gorer found that 51 per cent of the upper middle class respondents claimed no experience of intercourse prior to marriage, as against only 29 per cent from the non-skilled manual strata.[20] American investigators, with characteristic diligence, have discovered that whilst prolonging adolescence and delaying marriage, middle class young people often become skilled in a repertoire of 'pre-coital techniques' with which the working classes are likely to remain completely unfamiliar.[21] Between the two world wars a practice known as 'dating' developed amongst American college students. It subsequently spread through the high school population and was exported to other countries including Britain. Today dating is an out-of-date concept, but the type of relationship in question, where unlike 'courtship' marriage is not necessarily anticipated, and which can be freely terminated by either party, remains prevalent. Experience of this type of relationship, however, is still most extensive amongst middle class young people. They are the more likely to experience a series of relationships with some emotional depth prior to forming liaisons with the partners they eventually marry. Working class teenagers are less likely to 'play the market' in a comparable manner. They drift into engagements, marry at younger ages, and apart from their spouses, may otherwise experience only casual, pick-up affairs.

Following courtship and its antecedents, marriage and homemaking offer contrasting experiences at different levels in the social scale, and before drifting to the lofty realms of social psychology it is worth emphasizing that many of these differences are due to money – the economic circumstances of families. Working class couples do not embark upon marriage with the financial assets that the middle classes often have at their disposal. The former marry younger and their parents are unlikely to possess substantial capital sums to hand down the generations. In his study of *Middle Class Families* Colin Bell has drawn attention to the financial assistance that middle aged, middle class parents are able to offer to grown-up, recently-married children.[22] A deposit on a house or a central heating system may be considered suitable wedding gifts. The arrival of grandchildren often occasions further generosity – gifts of prams, furnished nurseries and expensive toys for Christmas. Middle class earnings peak in middle age, enabling grandparents to subsidise the living standards of the next generation. Working class home-making rarely benefits from this scale of assistance.

Hannah Gavron's study of *The Captive Wife* illustrates how couples' circumstances and problems depend upon their social class positions.[23] This study was based upon interviews with over 80 wives with young children, all living in North London, but in different social strata. A Hampstead group of 35 middle class wives was selected from doctors' lists and the Housewives' Register, and compared with 48 working class wives from Kentish Town. As the title indicates, Gavron's book is concerned with the predicament of the home-bound, captive wife, and these problems transcend class boundaries. But Gavron's evidence illustrates how middle class mothers are usually better positioned to climb on top of their circumstances. It was the working class mothers who became hopelessly trapped. Gavron's middle class wives were mainly living in independent houses and flats which were being purchased on mortgages. The working class families were mostly in rented rooms in multi-occupied property. For their captive wives, the middle class homes were comfortable prisons. The working class accommodation was comparatively oppressive. It is difficult to emulate the ideal wife in the television advertisements when sharing a bathroom, and when the kitchen is a converted landing. Gavron's middle class mothers were older and had commenced parenthood later than their working class counterparts. Eighty-five per cent claimed that their children were planned, meaning that the couples had consciously decided that they wanted children before conception. In contrast, 71 per cent of the working class births were said to be unplanned, though rarely unwanted. The practice of birth control is now normal at all levels in the social scale, but Gavron's research suggests persisting differences in its use. Amongst her working class couples, birth control was used 'negatively' – to prevent more children arriving when the wives felt they had produced enough. Parenthood was not a status deliberately achieved. It was rather treated as an inevitable and early sequel to marriage. A further contrast was that the middle class wives had usually received some occupational training, and looked forward to eventually returning to work. The working class wives' experience was typically confined to unskilled jobs. They expected an eventual return to work but were not anticipating liberation. Working class women have not recently won the right to work. They have worked in factories ever since the industrial revolution and have never regarded it as a privilege. This is one reason why the rhetoric of *women's lib* fails to strike a chord amongst working class women.

Money is not the sole source of social class differences in family life. Within the working class the child-rearing phase is long recognized as a period when families face difficulties, and in traditional communities extended kinship systems have operated as important sources of help. A network of local relatives who can pop in and out of each other's houses furnishes a constant flow of sociability and friendship. In addition, more material assistance can flow from kinship, as when grandparents mind children whose mothers work. As explained above, traditional working class communities are in nation-wide decline and, as is increasingly typical, Gavon's wives were not surrounded by long-established kinship and neighbourhood networks. Few enjoyed daily contact with relatives, as was also the case amongst the middle class couples. In such 'privatized' circumstances, neighbours sometimes act as substitutes, but Gavron's working class wives proved the less adept at cultivating relationships with neighbours. Amongst the middle class wives, 69 per cent reported contact with neighbours whereas only 29 per cent of the working class wives did so. Some of the latter were leading highly cloistered lives. Seventy-nine per cent said that they watched television every single evening.[24] They rarely went out socially except as 'a couple', and to understand this reticence we only need to realize that the typical working class mother was once a working class child in a working class family living in a working class district, who went to a local primary school and then to the local secondary modern with her primary school friends. She left school at fifteen or sixteen to work in a local factory with other girls from her school. Shortly afterwards she drifted into love and thenceforward 'went out' with a single fellow. During childhood and early adolescence she was surrounded by friends amongst whom she mixed with effortless sociability. These friends were always and simply 'there'. During courtship, childhood friendships are allowed to wither, and particularly when marriage involves a move to accommodation in a new area, the wife can be left isolated at home with her children.

Growing up middle class is different. The family is more likely to be geographically mobile, especially if the father is pursuing a 'spiralist' career. Education is likely to involve attendance at a non-neighbourhood grammar school and thereafter at a non-local university or college, and school and college leavers seeking middle class jobs are the more likely to find work away from the areas where they were brought up. Musgrove has described how this middle class preparation for life supplies a training in meeting people and making friends – social skills that individuals retain throughout their lives.[25] Sinking roots in a totally new neighbourhood, starting from scratch by joining associations or going to evening classes and meeting new people, require social skills that are not acquired in communities where everyone mingles effortlessly. Hence the predicament of Gavron's captive working class wives, whose existences were encapsulated by their homes and children.

Work, social class values and family life

In addition to differences resulting from families' immediate social and economic circumstances, middle and working class environments harbour contrasting values with further implications for family life. Two important books have argued this theme, neither based upon British evidence, but if their arguments possess any validity they cannot be other than relevant in contemporary Britain.

D. G. McKinley's *Social Class and Family Life*[26] starts with the observation that manual employees are denied status at work. They are constantly on the receiving end of authority and their work is menial rather than prestigious. Unlike the middle class husband, the blue-collar employee cannot carry esteem and eminence from work into his home. According to McKinley, manual work's low status has profound implications for the male's orientations towards his roles as husband and father. Middle class husbands can use the emotional rewards, particularly the respect, that is attached to their jobs to secure their status and exercise authority at home. The manual worker has to adopt different strategies and may feel a need to compensate at home for the status deprivation experienced at work. One reaction that McKinley discusses produces the authoritarian husband/father, who bullies his family with verbal aggression and physical punishment, demanding obedience from children whilst remaining aloof from the emotional details of domestic life. Another reaction results in the withdrawn husband who retreats from home life, seeks companionship and emotional satisfactions amongst his mates, and leaves the management of the household and the care of children to his wife. In either case, one consequence is the mother becoming the centre for emotional life in the home. Hence the archetypal working class 'mum', the symbol of love and affection, whilst the father remains harsh or distant, or both. Middle class spouses are likely to develop more evenly balanced emotional relationships, resulting in 'companionate' or 'colleague' styles of marriage in which the partners play similar roles in the care and upbringing of children.

Although his argument is partly speculative, McKinley's theory is consistent with observed social class differences in family behaviour in Britain, and illustrates how the effects of work cannot be encapsulated within the work situation. Roach[27] has sensibly warned against exaggerating the significance of status frustration to the neglect of constraints associated with the material facts of working class life. Acknowledging the latter's importance, however, does not require a denial of the socio-psychological processes to which McKinley draws attention.

The second study, M. Kohn's *Class and Conformity*,[28] is based upon detailed research in Turin and Washington supplemented by information from a national sample of American males, and is of particular interest in demonstrating how class variations in family life cut across national boundaries. The central point of interest in Kohn's study concerns the values that parents seek to develop in their children and how these relate to the techniques used in controlling the children's behaviour. The main contrast that Kohn's research highlights is the emphasis that middle class parents place upon self-direction – requiring children to acquire independence and control their own behaviour in approved ways. In working class households more emphasis is placed upon conformity – training children to do as they are told. In both Italy and the USA, Kohn found middle class parents responding to their children's *intentions*; looking behind overt behaviour to identify and approve or disapprove of the motives, and communicating with children to explain carefully why some types of behaviour were considered right and others wrong. Working class parents tended to respond to the immediate *consequences* of a child's behaviour. There was less concern with intentions and motives. The emphasis was rather upon punishing behaviour considered unacceptable. Why should manual and non-manual parents behave so differently? As in McKinley's theory, Kohn's data spotlighted the parents' experience at work as the discriminating factor. Opportunities to be self-directed at work emerged as especially important. Middle class parents enjoyed such opportunities, learnt to value self-direction and autonomy, and consequently aimed to encourage these qualities in their children. In working class jobs the emphasis is upon obedience and following instructions. Their jobs teach working class adults that 'Ours is not to reason why', and these attitudes penetrate their homes. As will become evident in the next chapter, these social class variations in child-rearing carry implications for children's behaviour in school, and hence for their future life-chances.

In Britain one of the most informative investigations into family life and child-rearing has been conducted by John and Elizabeth Newson.[29] Their enquiry, based upon a sample of over 700 Nottingham mothers who were interviewed when their children were still infants and again at age four, had mainly descriptive rather than theoretical objectives.

The prime intention was simply to discover how parents really do treat their children. However, the social class contrasts revealed are consistent with the theories outlined above. Class differences in styles of parenthood were evident even before the children's births. Middle class mothers were older, made the greater use of ante-natal services and were the more likely to arrange for the births to occur in maternity hospitals. These contrasts reinforce Gavron's observations about the more purposive approach to child-bearing amongst the middle classes. By the time the children were aged one, substantial class differences in child-rearing had appeared. These differences are illustrated in Table 4.1 which summarizes some of the evidence collected and compares the highest and lowest social class groups that the Newsons distinguished. Amongst working class parents, there was what at first might appear a contradictory combination of indulgence and punitive discipline. Working class mothers indulged their infants in being the more likely to use 'dummies' and allowing their children to use the 'bottle' beyond their first birthdays. At the same time, the working class mothers smacked their children the more frequently. Certain types of behaviour that were considered 'bad' including genital play were strictly prohibited and punished. The middle class husbands were the more 'highly participant', which is further evidence of the working class father's tendency to treat children as the mother's concern. Working class husbands were also the least likely to have been out socially with their wives during the year prior to the interviews. This type of companionship was more common amongst the Nottingham middle classes.

By the time the children were four years old these differences had matured into contrasting styles of parenthood. The less indulgent middle class parents were controlling the wider range of their children's behaviour. They were the more likely to intervene in quarrels between their own and other children, and to have definite rules about bedtime and table manners. In enforcing these rules the middle class parents tended to rely upon emotional sanctions – expressions of love and disapproval. They also considered it important to talk to their children and to explain the reasons behind rules, which is consistent with Kohn's argument about the middle class concern with 'intent'.

Table 4.1 Social class differences in child rearing (in percentages)

	No bottle at twelve months	Do not smack the child	Check genital play	Fathers rated 'highly participant'
Registrar-General's Social Classes 1 and 2 (upper white-collar strata)	50	56	25	57
Registrar-General's Social Class 5 (unskilled manual)	15	35	93	36

Source. J. and E. Newson, *Infant Care in an Urban Community*, Allen and Unwin, London, 1963.

Within working class homes, in one sense discipline was relatively lax. Children were given more freedom. When playing with friends they were expected to 'stand on their own feet', to 'stick up' for themselves, and even to 'hit back' when necessary. But once the consequences of the children's behaviour became a nuisance, working class parents were ready to descend with punitive discipline. There was less emphasis upon explaining why. Parents expected children to conform, 'Because I tell you'.

We know a great deal about the biological processes in which parents pass on traits through the genes. As yet we do not understand the mechanisms as thoroughly, but comparable process of social inheritance can be discerned. Patterns of behaviour can be preserved and handed down the generations through social learning processes. Looking onwards from the pre-school years, we can see how working class children enter their 'brief flowering period' of adolescence when parents abandon punitive control. And by this time, as will become fully evident in the next chapter, former working class children are mostly destined to become working class adults and parents. In this way the family acts as a key link in reproducing the class structure.

The Working Class

Are blue-collar life-styles distinctly working class?

For the purpose of differentiating courtship, home-making and child-rearing practices, social class is an inexact concept. As with other social class differences, there are exceptions to every generalization, and there is certainly no clean division between the working and middle classes. The sharpness of most of the contrasts presented above can be justified only when juxtaposing an upper middle against a lower working class. Despite the changes that have overtaken traditional working class patterns of community and family life, being a housewife, husband or child is not just the same in Chorley as in Chelsea. On this the evidence is clear. The interesting questions, however, concern the *extent* to which family and community life are affected by social class. Secondly, and crucially in the present discussion, in respect of the social class differences that do exist, is the middle–working class boundary a particularly marked point of variation?

Table 4.2 Mothers aged under 21 at birth of first child (in percentages)

Social class	
1 and 2	24
3 NM	25
3 M	40
4	46
5	53

Source. J. and E. Newson, *Infant Care in an Urban Community*, Allen and Unwin, London, 1963.

Whether the blue–white collar division acts as a watershed depends upon the aspects of family and community life under consideration. When we examine typical ages for marriage and the advent of parenthood, we find a step-by-step decline down the occupational hierarchy, but the biggest step coincides with the boundary between the middle and working classes (see Table 4.2). This is explicable in terms of the different career patterns of blue- and white-collar employees. The former usually leave full-time education at the earliest opportunity and achieve adult rates of pay early in their careers. White-collar careers are more likely to follow a full-time education in excess of the statutory minimum, and in the initial stages of their working lives individuals tend to be remunerated at the foot of salary scales which rise progressively with age.

Table 4.3 Housing and social class, 1971 (in percentages)

	Social class					
	1	2	3	4	5	6
Privately rented	12	17	22	17	25	23
Council	3	10	20	38	44	56
Owner-occupier	85	74	59	45	31	21

Source. General Household Survey Introductory Report, HMSO, London, 1973.

Types of housing vary between every step in the occupational hierarchy but once again, the transition between the white-collar and manual strata is a major juncture. Table 4.3 shows that at this level in descending the class structure owner-occupation ceases to be the majority status. Approximately a third of all blue-collar families do own their homes, and this proportion has been increasing throughout the post-war years. However, for manual families there are barriers to owner-occupation that the middle classes find easier to surmount. The capital required as deposit is more likely to flow down the middle class generations. Furthermore, with their relative security of employment and incremental salaries, white-collar workers are better able to commit themselves to mortgage repayments extending through the greater part of their working lives. For these same reasons, middle class applicants are likely to meet favourable responses from building societies. Social class values are also relevant. Within the middle classes home-ownership is a taken-for-granted aspiration. Home-ownership is a far from uncommon aspiration amongst blue-collar couples, but their own family backgrounds are less likely to make this a 'matter of fact' expectation. Realistic home-making plans are more likely to focus upon council housing, and in this market bargaining power is enhanced not by delaying parenthood and accumulating savings, but by having children and accumulating the 'points' to advance up the housing list.

It is unnecessary to exaggerate social class contrasts. In child-care practices there are huge similarities across all levels in the social hierarchy. Since the 1950s breast-feeding has been fashionable – applauded by women's magazines and encouraged by doctors and health visitors. Hence in all the social classes that Davie and his colleagues distinguished,[30] the majority of children were breast-fed for some time. It is nevertheless interesting that, as evident in Table 4.4, deviance from this norm increased as the social ladder was descended, and most sharply between the white- and blue-collar strata. All children are eventually weaned from both breast and bottle, but again it is significant that in the Newsons' enquiry the pace of this aspect of child development slowed substantially at the boundary beneath the middle class (See Table 4.4).

Table 4.4 Child-care practices

	Social class					
	1	2	3(NM)	3(M)	4	5
Percentage of children *not* breast-fed*	21	26	24	33	35	36
Percentages of mothers using a bottle when child aged 1†		50	53	71	79	85

*From R. Davie et al., *From Birth to Seven*, Longman, London, 1972.
† From J. & E. Newson, *Infant Care in an Urban Community*, Allen and Unwin, London, 1963.

Family, community and life-styles

Despite the above evidence, it is possible to focus upon aspects of family behaviour where, although there are changes between the top and bottom of the social scale, there is little variation at the point of transition from the white-collar to manual strata. In some cases it is an upper middle class that is markedly different from the rest, whilst in others a lower working class proves exceptional. For example, when the Newsons questioned their sample of mothers about reactions to infants' genital play, little difference was apparent between the lower middle and upper working classes, whereas the upper middle class proved especially libertarian and the lower working class exceptionally strict. Likewise the frequency with which four-year-old children were smacked varied little between the upper working and lower middle classes, but upper middle class children were exceptionally likely to escape physical punishment completely, whilst lower working class children were smacked with unusual frequency.

Some commentators consider mortality rates to be particularly sensitive indicators of the general quality of life, and in all age groups there is overall negative correlation between mortality and social class. When we ask where the rate rises most sharply, as Tables 4.5 and 4.6 illustrate, it is not between the middle and the working classes, but amongst the unskilled manual strata.

Table 4.5 Infant mortality rates, Scotland 1973

Social class	
1	12 per 1,000
2	14 " "
3	18 " "
4	18 " "
5	32 " "

Source. Registrar General for Scotland, *Annual Report for Scotland 1973*, HMSO, Edinburgh, 1974.

Table 4.6 Mortality rates 1959–63, men age 55–64

Social class	
1	1,699 per 100,000
2	1,820 " "
3	2,218 " "
4	2,208 " "
5	2,912 " "

Source. Registrar General, *Decennial Supplement, England and Wales, 1961,* HMSO, London, 1971.

Recorded delinquency is a further type of behaviour that rises gradually as the occupational hierarchy is descended without any unusually large increase between the white- and blue-collar strata. Douglas' follow-up study of a sample of children born during March 1946 found that by their seventeenth birthdays over 20 per cent of those with non-skilled manual fathers had been convicted by the courts or cautioned by the police, and the difference between this group's delinquency and its prevalence amongst the skilled manual strata was as great as between the latter and the level recorded amongst boys from lower middle class homes (see Table 4.7).[31] Ecological studies, which compare crime rates in particular districts, reveal a concentration in 'slum' areas. Working class districts do not display uniform crime rates. Rather is official criminality concentrated in notorious areas, which in some cases have retained their reputations over generations.[32] West and Farrington's research which followed the progress of 411 schoolboys from a working class area in London from age 8 to 19 found that the fifth who became official delinquents tended to be from the larger, low-income families, often with parents possessing criminal records and whose standards of child-rearing were judged unsatisfactory.[33]

The terms 'official' and 'recorded' delinquency have been used in the above discussion since it is known that only a fraction of all crimes committed reach police and court records. Official statistics suggest that crime is a minority activity, whereas studies inviting respondents to anonymously confess reveal high rates of admitted delinquency in all sections of the population. Most young people commit petty property offences and minor crimes against the person. Amongst adults traffic offences and minor thefts from work are so common that they are rarely considered 'real' crime. Faced with this evidence, Box and Ford have argued that 'the facts don't fit',[34] that crime is not related to social class in the way that official statistics suggest and theoreticians have supposed. They argue that the apparent relationship in official records can be explained in terms of biased reporting, police and court practices. Blytheway and May[35] propose caution before jettisoning the conventional wisdom, and argue that at least some facts do fit. Amongst women they agree that it is impossible to discern a consistent relationship between self-reported crime and social class, and for adult males they recommend suspending judgement in view of the sparse evidence. For young males, however, they insist that the conventional wisdom holds. This accords with McDonald's findings amongst 900 fourth formers in twelve secondary schools.[36] There were high rates of admitted delinquency amongst boys from all strata, but the most frequent offenders were from the foot of the social scale.

Table 4.7 Percentages of boys with criminal records by age 17

Father's occupation	
Professional	5·0
Salaried	4·5
Self-employed	9·0
Blackcoated	10·3
Foreman/skilled	15·1
Semi-skilled	20·1
Unskilled	20·6
Agricultural	14·6

Source. J. W. B. Douglas et al., 'Delinquency and Social Class', *British Journal of Criminology*, 6 (1966) 294–302.

For purposes of the present discussion it is unnecessary to establish the social contours of delinquency with the precision that criminologists seek. The key point is that in so far as there is a relationship between criminality and social class, it is not the kind of relationship that we find, for example, in party political loyalties which juxtapose the white- and blue-collar strata. Both official statistics and self-reported studies indicate a concentration of persistent and relatively serious criminality amongst a lower working class.

Members of the working class are well aware of the difference between the 'rough' and 'respectable'. In most urban areas there are certain districts, even streets and families, which have acquired notoriety, whilst other districts are considered 'desirable' by 'decent' families. Elias and Scotson's interviews and participant observation in a suburb of a midlands city illustrates how sharply these distinctions can be made, and how persistent reputations can become once acquired.[37] Within the suburb that was investigated residents distinguished three neighbourhoods that were arranged in a status hierarchy. The most prestigious was occupied mainly by middle class households. It was followed by a respectable working class area that had a history stretching from the end of the nineteenth century. The third neighbourhood had a shorter history. In its early days it had acquired an unsavoury reputation. Its initial inhabitants included a handful of 'problem families' who earned the entire district a reputation as rough and undesirable. The inhabitants were never accepted as social equals by other locals, and were aware of the low status attached to their own estate. They resented the superior pretensions of residents in other districts, but could feel little identity or attachment to their own neighbourhood. Elias and Scotson describe in detail how young people respond to life in such an area. They were not controlled by local pressures towards respectability. Indeed, attitudes in the surrounding society defined a 'rough' status in which 'outsider' boys were expected to excel, and many responded.

Divorce is a crude measure of family instability, but Gibson's[38] analysis of the available data reveals two peaks; one amongst the lower white-collar strata, the other in the unskilled working class. The former peak is explicable in terms of the age composition of the group. The risk of divorce is greatest during a marriage's initial decade of life, before non-manual employees have begun to climb their career ladders into the higher occupational strata. The high rate of divorce amongst unskilled manual families is not explicable in such terms. It is rather a further indication of social disorganization amongst the lower working class.

From within industry the sharpest and most visible break in the social hierarchy separates the working class from superordinate strata. In contrast, looking outwards from the homes and through the communities in which the more skilled and better paid manual workers live, the differences between their own respectable lives and the circumstances of the 'roughs' are often more apparent. In terms of how people live, differences between the lower middle and upper working class are overwhelmed by the similarities. Family Expenditure Surveys show that the average disposable incomes of manual and lower-middle class households differ only marginally. As Table 4.8 shows, they spend their money in rather different ways. The middle class spends more on

Table 4.8 Household expenditure upon selected items

| | Occupational group | | |
	Professional	Clerical (in £'s)	Manual
Housing	9·3	7·3	5·7
Fuel, light, power	2·7	2·3	2·3
Food	13·0	10·9	12·6
Alcohol	2·4	2·1	2·8
Clothing, footwear	5·2	4·4	4·6
Transport	10·8	6·4	6·6
Total	63·2	48·0	48·3

Source. Department of Employment, *Family Expenditure Survey, Report for 1974*, HMSO, London, 1975.

housing, whilst manual households spend more on food and alcohol. These differences, however, pale into insignificance when both manual and lower-middle class households are compared with upper middle class families. The latter enjoy substantially greater spending power which supplies the basis for a distinct life-style, involving high levels of expenditure on housing and transport in particular.

Table 4.9 Social class and selected leisure activities (in percentages)

	Social class					
	1	2	3NM	3N	4	5
Visit public house at least once a month*	40	44	46	47		47
Drink 'frequently' at home †	77	58	44	45		25
Attend cinema once a month or more‡	15	14	14	12	11	4
Attend church once a month or more §	23		17	13	17	

*From M. Bradley and D. Fenwick, *Public Attitudes to Liquor Licensing Laws in Great Britain*, HMSO, London, 1974.

†Ibid.

‡National Opinion Polls, 1975.

§National Opinion Polls, 1972.

Across many areas of leisure behaviour social class differences are minute. For example, visits to public houses vary little in frequency between the top and bottom occupational groups. The BBC's audience research shows that the number of hours devoted to televiewing is greatest within group 'C' (mainly manual families); 19·3 hours in February 1973 as against only 15·1 hours in group 'A'. These differences, however, need to be set in the context of television acting as the most important single object of recreational behaviour in all social classes. Differences in leisure habits less frequently juxtapose the middle and working classes than separate upper middle and lower working classes from the middle mass of the population. For example, alcohol is most likely to be drunk frequently at home amongst the upper middle class, and church-going is also exceptionally common amongst this group. Unskilled manual families are distinguished, amongst other things, by rarely drinking alcohol at home, and rarely visiting the cinema (see Table 4.9). Although not wholly untrue, it is misleading to associate interest in 'high culture' with the middle class. When we examine, for example, the composition of theatre audiences it turns out to be a college-educated upper middle class that predominates,[39] and within this stratum a much greater volume of leisure time is devoted to television than high culture. When observers focus upon family and neighbourhood life-styles, they find cause to question the validity of the middle/working class dichotomy.

Male worker chauvinism and class analysis

Like most academic disciplines, sociology has not escaped a touch of male chauvinism. The analyses of 'society' enshrined in 'the literature' are weighted with research on the male half of the population. Studies of delinquency, the transition into employment and perhaps social class in particular give pride of place to male behaviour and attitudes. Dichotomizing the population into working and middle classes using occupation as an index is at best an oversimplification of reality, albeit one that can be justified as drawing attention to a major cleavage in the social structure. This justification, however, is most plausible when male workers are the subjects of analysis.

Discussions of social class sometimes forget that approximately half the population is economically inactive. In some instances it is reasonable to infer the interests and values of the inactive from their normal occupations. For example, the standards of living of the retired depend upon the fringe benefits attached to their previous jobs, and values developed during a life-time in employment can be expected to survive into old age. Likewise housewives' standards of living depend substantially upon their husbands' jobs. Its members' occupations cannot but affect a family as a whole. Children's experiences of home life depend upon their parents' social class positions. All this has been fully illustrated.

The fact remains, however, that the further we move from the point of economic production, and the more we focus on groups not directly involved in these processes, the more vague the contours of inequality rooted in the division of labour at work become. Styles of family life do vary between the working and middle classes, but the schism between the two is by no means as sharp as when conditions of employment are considered. Variations in family behaviour within both the middle and working classes are considerable, for families are affected by numerous influences, many of which do not directly depend upon their members' work roles.

Allocating women to social classes poses well known research problems, illustrated by the debate between the supporters of HOCCUP (classification by head of household's occupation) and those favouring ROCCUP (respondent's own occupation). The former insist that the family rather than the individual be treated as the basic unit for class analysis. How can members of the same family possess different class positions and interests? If we accept that the woman's main role is domestic, then irrespective of any job that she holds, her position in the class structure can be seen as depending upon her husband's occupation. Other analysts argue that for married women today employment has become a normal rather than an incidental activity, and that her own occupation should be used to assess a woman's class position. Neither method of categorization is incontrovertibly valid. Each has points in its favour, but both ride roughshod over some complexities of real life. Hollander[40] has pointed out that in western countries the status and treatment of women depends considerably upon their feminine characteristics, particularly their physical attractiveness, and this, Hollander correctly observes, has become a largely achieved status rather than ascribed by nature. If our examinations of stratification focused on the female half of the population we would have to pay more attention to this dimension of inequality than is accorded in most standard texts. For women, the dynamics of social mobility are not identical to the processes applying amongst men. Males improve their class positions through education and occupational success. Women's life-chances depend substantially upon who they marry, and this difference is reflected in teenagers' aspirations as regards the future.[41] Realizing a woman's aspirations requires its own strategies. The position of women in society is changing. There is a trend towards according women statuses that are not subservient to the domestic role. Yet especially within the working class, *women's lib* is still a radical idea rather than a reality,[42] and even amongst the middle classes there remains some foundation for the view that, for women, one of the attractions of college lies in its access to a desirable marriage market.

Contemporary society is sufficiently complex to contain interests and values that are not directly derived from the division of labour in the economy. Forty per cent of the men in Gorer's national sample defined themselves as working class, whereas only 26 per cent of female respondents did so.[43] Identifying oneself 'up' the social scale and with the middle class is more common amongst women. One explanation concerns the greater likelihood of female's own work experience being in the white-collar sector. Another concerns a tendency for women to see their positions in society in terms of the consumer rather than the producer role. If they can afford similar houses, furniture and holidays to middle class families, blue-collar wives will consider themselves as having risen above the working class. It is no coincidence that Ineichen's research,[44] that found considerable evidence of bourgeois attitudes and life-styles amongst blue-collar owner-occupiers, involved interviews with women, whereas *The Affluent Worker*[45] study whose findings were mainly critical of the embourgeoisement thesis was based primarily upon a male sample.

When sociologists insist that the white/blue-collar schism is a real cleavage in the social structure, they are unwise to pretend that *all* inequalities fall neatly away from this divide. Differences that do not juxtapose the working and middle classes are not difficult to discover. Ethnicity is a basis of discrimination, unequal treatment and, therefore, social stratification. The youth culture is pervaded by social class differences, but this cannot disguise the fact young people have interests and life-styles that distinguish them from other sections of the population. Likewise there are inequalities amongst the retired reflecting their former occupations, but there are senses in which all who are dependent upon state welfare possess interests that distinguish them from workers. Although its imprint never disappears, the further we move from the point of economic production, the fainter the cleavage between the middle and working classes becomes whilst other sources of inequality increase in prominence.

The evidence reviewed in this and the previous chapters offers little support for the argument that inequalities are being smoothed into continuous gradients resembling the functionalist model of stratification. On the other hand, the Weberian proposition that stratification is multi-dimensional finds considerable support. In contemporary Britain all inequalities do not fall into similar patterns. A manual working class is distinguished by the division of labour in industry, and the effects of inequalities rooted in the organization of the economy ripple into non-working life. However, when we examine family and community behaviour, we discover that the contours of these ripples are often submerged in social differences with other bases. Focusing upon the population's life-styles outside work offers no grounds for alleging classlessness, and differences between the manual and white-collar strata remain in evidence, but the middle–working class schism does not consistently present itself as the main point of contrast. The further we move from the work situation, the more the utility of the working class concept diminishes.

Education

Class origins and life-chances

In the 1930s poverty and fee-paying were the emotive issues in the education debate. Through the trade unions and Labour Party the cry had been raised for equality of opportunity. What stood in the way? Firstly poverty; children who were ill-clothed, under-nourished and whose parents, even given the right, could not afford to support them through secondary school. Secondly the cost of secondary education; children whose parents could pay were virtually guaranteed access to a (frequently subsidized) secondary school irrespective of ability, whilst the remainder faced the scholarship hurdle.

Following the Second World War a new era was intended to dawn. The welfare state was to abolish poverty by casting a safety net beneath which no citizen would fall. For the most needy families financial support was to assist children to complete their schooling. In addition to free school meals, grants could be made towards the cost of uniforms, and further support became available if children continued their education beyond the minimum leaving age. Young people who qualified for university became eligible for maintenance grants as of right. Simultaneously, after the 1944 Education Act, fee-paying was abolished in local authority schools. Subsequently only a limited number of direct-grant schools were allowed to retain their independence and admit fee-paying pupils whilst receiving support from public funds, a privileged status that began to be phased out under the 1974 Labour government. The 1944 Act decreed secondary education for all, of a type suited to each child's ability and aptitude; the social and financial status of a child's family were deemed irrelevant to educational opportunity.

How ill-founded this optimism proved. Since 1944 researchers have assiduously documented how social class remains relevant to children's chances at virtually every stage in what was intended to be a socially impartial educational process. When ability grouping is practised, working class children tend to be allocated to the lower streams in primary schools.[1] When the 11-plus was in general operation, segregating children into grammar and secondary modern schools, working class children were under-represented in the former.[2] Whether in grammar schools or secondary moderns, it is the working class children who sink downstream.[3] Children from middle class homes are the more likely to continue beyond O-levels into sixth forms, then beyond A-levels into higher education.[4] Within higher education in Britain social origins are unrelated to success. University students from working class homes obtain equivalent results to their middle class peers.[5] But before an age group enters higher education social class disparities in attainment are extremely wide. Amongst children born during 1940–1, and therefore educated following the 1944 Act, 33 per cent of those with fathers in higher professional and administrative occupations entered full-time degree level courses, whilst only 1 per cent from non-skilled manual families did so. In contrast, only 7 per cent from the top social class obtained no educational qualifications whatsoever, compared with 65 per cent from non-skilled working class families (see Table 5.1).

What is disillusioning is not just the persistence of social class inequalities, but that they have narrowed only marginally if at all. Since the 1930s, the proportion of all university students from working class backgrounds has remained fairly constant at between 25 and 30 per cent. Successive innovations have been heralded with hopes of improving working class children's prospects, only for the idealism to turn sour. Instead of offering a fair chance, the 11-plus procedures soon attracted criticism of bias against working class children. More recently, within comprehensive schools it has proved to be the working class pupils who move downstream whilst others progress through O-levels.[6] Likewise the growth of opportunities for higher level studies in further education since 1966 with the designation of Polytechnics has been exploited mainly by the middle classes. Two-thirds of all students on degree courses in the Polytechnics come from white-collar homes.[7]

We must confess some ignorance of precise up-to-the-minute trends. Following any educational change, we must wait until an age group has entered and passed through the system before the full impact can become evident. In the latest national study of social mobility in Britain, the youngest respondents were born in 1949. Their chances of upward mobility can be systematically compared with earlier generations. The effects of more recent educational trends, including the demise of the 11-plus, can be assessed with less precision. Using data from the latest national study, Halsey has compared the educational attainments of individuals born between 1930 and 1949, with those born during the previous twenty years.[8] The evidence shows that at each extreme of the social scale inequalities have been reduced.

Table 5.1 Highest educational level, by social class of father, attained by children born in 1940–1 in Great Britain (in percentages)

| | Registrar General's social class | | | | | |
	I	II	IIINM	IIIM	IV and V	All
Degree-level, full-time higher education	33	11	6	2	1	4
No post-school course, or 'O' levels, or Scottish Leaving Certificate	7	20	29	49	65	47

Derived from Table 2, Higher Education, 1963, Appendix 1, Part 2, Section 2.

The advantages of upper middle class children relative to the lower middle class have narrowed, and likewise with the disadvantages of the non-skilled relative to the skilled working class. But the disparity in attainment between the lower middle and upper working classes has remained unchanged, and 'the statistics show the steepness of the remaining inequality, with upper middle class children having three times an average chance (of entering higher education) and the lower working class having less than half the average chance. . . . So much for the progress of educational opportunity'.

Two follow-through enquiries, based upon samples born in 1946[9] and 1958[10] respectively, have charted the persistence of unequal attainments, and recent studies of prestigious occupations reveal little progress towards equal opportunity. Boyd collected information about élite office-holders in the civil service, foreign service, judiciary, armed services, Church of England and clearing banks in 1939, 1950, 1960 and 1971.[11] Public school and Oxbridge backgrounds predominated and, except in the civil service, there was no trend over time towards ex-public schoolboys becoming less prominent. We may be unable to quantify the *precise* extent to which children's chances of success still depend upon the strata into which they are born, but we can be confident that this extent remains considerable.

Educational opportunity arouses widespread concern because its importance extends beyond education. Amongst other roles, education is now an apparatus of occupational selection. Degrees and other certificates unlock job prospects, and failure in education restricts a wider range of life-chances. Recognition that education had become the route to advantageous job opportunities fuelled the pre-1944 campaign for equal access to secondary schools, and the continuing under-representation of children from working class origins in the higher reaches of education means that they still have a much less than equal chance of achieving middle class status. Because education is more than an end in itself, relativities are as important as absolute levels of attainment. In absolute terms, educational opportunities have widened for everyone, so working class children today have a greater chance than their parents of obtaining O- and A-levels, and eventually entering higher education. However, this also applies amongst the middle classes. Working class pupils continue to be out-distanced, and this persistent state of affairs concerns a wide body of opinion. Part of this concern stems from a belief that social and economic efficiency would increase if talent was fully exploited, irrespective of its origins.

Overriding this, however, is a conviction that the current distribution of educational and related life-chances is simply unfair.

It is naive to pretend that the persistence of inequalities is attributable to the ill-intent of policy-makers and implementers. The plain fact is that no one knows how to establish equal opportunity. There are plenty of ideas on offer, but with no greater guarantee of success than their many predecessors. Social class inequalities in education are not confined to Britain. In every society for which information is available, industrial and non-industrial, capitalist and socialist, these inequalities are repeated. Compared with other Western European countries, working class children in Britain possess an unusually good chance of eventually reaching university. Our inability to supply answers reflects the disagreement as to why working class children are unsuccessful. We are now aware that poverty and fee-paying were never the only obstacles. What other factors impede working class children?

Intelligence

One school of thought attributes working class children's poor performances at school to a lack of intelligence; a point of view surrounded by controversy which arises not only over interpretations of the evidence, but more so over the implications that follow. Much of the argument hinges upon the status of intelligence tests and the intelligence quotients (IQ scores) that are derived. There is no dispute that children's measured intelligence correlates positively with social class. But so what?

'Hereditarians' believe that IQ tests measure innate ability. They argue that one of the most important facts about intelligence is that we *can* measure it despite considerable ignorance of exactly how it is bred.[12] IQ scores, it is claimed, correlate with success in all tasks requiring mental ability including school-work. The opposing point of view queries whether IQ tests really measure intelligence in the sense that the term is ordinarily understood. At the extreme there are arguments that IQ scores indicate little more than an ability to complete intelligence tests. The more moderate opposition argues that whilst the tests are reasonably accurate for predicting success in school, they are less efficient when predicting success in other spheres including occupations, which depends upon many other environmental and personality factors. A low IQ score, therefore, is considered a poor excuse for labelling a child as 'unable'.

As the name implies, 'hereditarians' stress the importance of genetic as opposed to environmental determinants of intelligence. Some writers claim that genetic factors account for 80 per cent of the variation in IQ scores between individuals. 'Environmentalists' regard these figures as highly suspect. They stress that we cannot directly measure innate ability. By the time that individuals become testable, complex processes of interaction between nature and nurture have occurred, and the contributions of these sets of influences are not easily separated.[13]

If only a scientific problem was at issue the two sides would no doubt see the merits in each other's arguments and recognize that the matters of fact in dispute are questions of degree.[14] However, apart from scientific truth, educational policy is at stake. 'Hereditarians' protest that it is pointless for education to try to overcome nature. Educational practices need to recognize differences in ability. Practices that fail to take intelligence differences into account, such as refusing to group children by ability for teaching purposes, are therefore opposed. If the outcome appears to favour middle class children, so be it. Although there is considerable overlapping and a wide spread of intelligence amongst children born into all strata, 'hereditarians' conclude that we must ultimately reconcile ourselves to the evidence that, on the whole, working class children are less able than others. To 'environmentalists' these implications are anathema. They argue that IQ scores have insufficient validity as measures of genuine potential to be employed in a way that turns their predictions into self-fulfilling prophecies. We may not know *exactly* how much of the variation in attainment amongst schoolchildren can be attributed to environmental factors, but it is argued that environment is known to exert some influence, and whilst we cannot change individuals' genes, we can do something about their environments. The 'environmentalists' urge, therefore, that education should consistently strive to develop each individual's potential, and that the under-achievement of working class children should be regarded as a challenge rather than a fact of life to which we must resign ourselves. Working class children's performances on IQ tests and their classroom attainments could both be depressed by the same environmental forces. It is alleged that using IQ to 'explain' working class under-achievement is an ideological rather than a purely scientific judgement. Employing their superior IQ scores to justify socio-educational arrangements that work to the net advantage of the middle classes legitimizes what would otherwise be recognized and condemned as unfair.[15]

In an overall review of the social class–educational attainment relationship, it is necessary to keep the debate about intelligence in perspective. There is no need to appraise all the studies that have compared the IQ scores of identical as against fraternal twins reared together and apart, nor to examine the claims of tests that purport to be relatively culture-fair. No 'hereditarian' seeks to deny that environment has some effect on both IQ scores and school performance, and a desire to stress their own subject's relevance need not lead sociologists to claim that *all* differences in attainment between individuals are consequences of their social environments. Everyday experience in addition to the results of IQ tests indicates that individuals do differ in their ability to handle schoolwork, and it would be surprising if the abilities conducive to success at school had absolutely nothing to do with genetic endowment. Brain-damaged and sub-normal children cannot be explained away in environmental terms, and these cases are not odd instances but the end of a continuum. In so far as mental ability is amongst the factors explaining success in life, its distribution amongst the adult population must be expected to correlate with social class, and likewise its distribution amongst children in so far as ability is partly genetically determined. Their strength and importance can be disputed, but it is difficult to argue that these processes have nothing what-soever to contribute to explaining working class children's school performances.

Even the most militant 'hereditarians' admit that genetics cannot explain the whole scale on which working class children under-achieve. Even when their IQ scores are identical, in general middle class children out-perform their working class counterparts. Under the 11-plus system, middle class children were the more likely to obtain grammar school places even with IQ held constant.[16] If we credit IQ tests with offering at least a crude measure of ability, then we have conclusive evidence that the failure of working class children is not *entirely* due to an innate lack of talent. If the 'hereditarian' interpretation of IQ is dismissed wholesale, it becomes impossible to ascertain that working class children are under-achieving relative to their own potential. Agnosticism becomes the only rational inference, and this is surely untenable given the overall weight of the evidence. The surveys conducted by the Crowther Committee[17] in the late 1950s revealed that over four out of every ten young people in the top 10 per cent of the measured ability range were leaving full-time education before their sixteenth birthdays. These 'drop-outs' were mainly from working class families. Hence the Crowther Report's tirade against education's failure to drain the 'pool of ability' and the resulting 'wastage of talent'. We can be confident that social influences impair working class children's educational progress, but only if we do not completely dismiss the hereditarian argument.

Social class values

As we have seen, in the immediate aftermath of 1944 it was widely believed that equal opportunity had arrived. This optimism evaporated during the 1950s as a succession of reports demonstrated that the Act's impact had been less dramatic than anticipated, and this disillusion inspired further research to explain why. One school of thought stressed working class children's limited intellectual potential, but in sociology the favoured explanation emphasized social handicaps. Working class children were seen as held back not by the naked economic barriers that had been prominent in the past but by 'cultural deprivation', as these handicaps became described. Investigators identified a syndrome of working class values which impeded children's progress. Working class parents were found to possess lower educational and occupational aspirations in comparison with the middle classes. In addition, working class parents were less knowledgeable about the educational system. They were less familiar with the subjects their children were studying, particularly in secondary schools, and less aware of the opportunities available beyond the statutory leaving age. Related to this, working class parents appeared to take little active interest in their children's education. They were the less likely to visit schools to discuss their children's work with teachers. In contrast, middle class parents communicated high aspirations and actively encouraged their children towards them. In this sense, for middle class children the values to which they were exposed at home and school were congruent and mutually supporting. Working class children were seen as comparatively handicapped or culturally deprived.

Boudon distinguishes these 'secondary' effects of stratification upon educational opportunity from 'primary' consequences that operate directly upon levels of attainment.[18] On all tests of ability or attainment, working class children are out-performed by the middle classes. Above and beyond this, however, at any given level of attainment working class children are the more likely to drop or be sifted from the educational system. They are the less likely to enter grammar schools, sit O-levels, stay on for A-levels, and so on. These consequences of stratification are secondary only in not operating directly on levels of attainment. Their effects are anything but trivial; they are extremely powerful since they operate exponentially. Working class disadvantages are multiplied at every educational hurdle and it is this, rather than crude inability, either inborn or environmentally bred, that accounts for the landslide scale of working class failure by the end of the educational process.

The theme of working class culture impeding children's progress at school was developed in early exploratory studies during the 1950s. Mays' study of *Education and the Urban Child*,[19] based upon evidence from a working class area in inner Liverpool, observed how the disinterest and apathy of parents could envelop a primary school, resulting in teachers resigning themselves to only the occasional 11-plus success. In *Education and the Working Class*,[20] Jackson and Marsden examined the case-histories of eighty-eight working class children who did rise towards the top of the educational tree by attending grammar schools, staying on and taking A-levels. These pupils were untypical of their working class peers not only in their success, but also in that their backgrounds resembled a 'sunken middle class' with many fathers in supervisory jobs and mothers who had 'married down'. Jackson and Marsden's analysis of the educational careers of these pupils highlighted a range of handicaps to which children from more solidly working class backgrounds would be a more powerfully subject. Parents who did not understand the education their children were receiving were ill placed to supply the help and encouragement that was available in the homes of ten middle class pupils who were studied for comparative purposes. Jackson and Marsden described how the success of the working class children, which was a source of pride to their parents, nevertheless drew the children away from their families, and their neighbourhood friends also. The culture of the school conflicted with attitudes to which the pupils were exposed at home and in their neighbourhoods, with the result that many children spoke of having to act like different people in these different environments. Middle class children do not have to break with the culture of their homes and neighbourhoods in order to enjoy educational success, and it was clear that the problems of Jackson and Marsden's working class students had not ended with their grammar school careers. Whilst becoming detached from the culture of their homes and neighbourhoods, the young people remained unassimilated into the middle classes. Many seemed to cling to school-work as their one secure foothold in life.

Recent studies conducted during the 1970s indicate how little has changed. Birksted's unusually detailed account of six fifteen-year-old boys at a comprehensive school near Brighton[21] describes how, for some young people, school fails to operate as a major organizing principle in their lives. It is accorded little importance compared with friends and future jobs. Birksted's boys regarded school as a kind of waiting room, a place for filling time. The boys recognized that school had a purpose for some people – those who could pass exams that would help them obtain jobs, but the backgrounds of Birksted's informants had not encouraged them to see their own futures in these terms. Greenslade's *Goodbye to the Working Class*[22] confirms how even its successes remain ambivalently served by the educational system. Ten years after leaving, Greenslade contacted over a hundred of his contemporaries at Dagenham County High School, an unusual grammar school in that its intake was mainly working class. As a result of their educational success, like Greenslade himself who became a journalist, most of the ex-pupils had 'got on' in obtaining better jobs and houses than their parents. However, rather than securely settled in the middle class, Greenslade felt it more appropriate to describe his subjects as a 'domesticated class' of uncritical conformists with shallow life-styles, whose interests and aspirations rarely extended beyond wall-to-wall carpeting and stereo equipment.

Since the 1950s research has constantly enlarged our understanding of how a working class background can depress children's achievements. Banks and Finlayson[23] studied 345 boys and their parents during their initial four years at a grammar school and in the academic streams of a secondary technical and a comprehensive school. Over- and under-achievers were distinguished in relation to predictions of future attainments based upon their performances at 11-plus. Characteristics of the over-achieving pupil included possessing high aspirations, intellectual curiosity and a compliant as opposed to rebellious disposition. This type of pupil was nurtured by a home background most common amongst the middle classes – where parents had high aspirations, warm and affectionate relationships with their children and where emotive techniques of discipline were the norm.

In terms of its influence upon educational policy, the most successful research has undoubtedly been that conducted on behalf of the Plowden Committee and incorporated in its report, *Children and their Primary Schools*.[24] This research involved over 3,000 children from a national sample of 173 primary schools and stressed the importance of home as opposed to school factors such as class size and teacher characteristics in explaining variations in achievement. Furthermore, as regards the home, the research emphasized the influence of attitudes, the interest and encouragement that parents offered as against material circumstances such as income and housing. A follow-up study four years later when the Plowden sample was in secondary education found all the expected relationships between the children's home backgrounds and their subsequent progress.[25] The Plowden Report argued that when children were otherwise handicapped by their social backgrounds, education should positively discriminate and make good the deficit. Hence the proposals, subsequently implemented, for Educational Priority Areas to which additional finance would be targeted. The Plowden Report also suggested measures aimed at replacing culture-conflict with supportive relationships between home and school; more contact between teachers and parents, and the appointment of social workers to liaise.

In an action research project in a London junior school, Young and McGeeney had already pioneered methods of improving home–school relationships.[26] The 'action' included open days with exhibitions of work, talks between parents and the head, class teachers and the librarian, meetings at which teaching methods were discussed and home visits by some teachers. During the lifetime of the project the IQ scores of the pupils improved, which was encouraging, but, as is always a problem with single case studies, whether this was due to the action in the project could not be conclusively proved.

The major steps towards operationalizing the Plowden philosophy occurred in another subsequent, government-sponsored action research project based upon five designated educational priority areas. The eventual report[27] describes a series of initiatives in pre-school and primary education which included applying the 'community school' concept in working class areas. Eric Midwinter, who directed the action research in Liverpool, declared, 'It is our ambition to make the social environment *the* "bread and butter" subject.'[28] The aim in community education is to break the cultural walls between the school and its locality. In the Liverpool project this meant encouraging pupils to study their local environment, displaying children's work in local shops, inviting parents into schools for coffee mornings and other functions, and producing school magazines. The intention, in the first instance, is to make education relevant to children and parents. This is seen as desirable in itself for, as Midwinter observers, the probability is that the majority of children in working class districts will remain in such areas, in which case it is desirable that education should help them to understand their milieux. Simultaneously, the intention is to trigger a chain reaction. It is hoped that a relevant curriculum and closer home–school relationships will result in parental attitudes pulling alongside rather than against the school, thereby raising levels of attainment.

This is the policy implication of analyses that identify the culture of the working class home and community, meaning the values, attitudes and interests that are transmitted to children, as a prime source of working class under-achievement. Somehow this culture has to be changed to remove the disadvantages it entails. 'Environmentalists' who insist that the culture of the home and neighbourhood inhibits the development of working class children's potential have mostly been optimistic about the prospects for change, but their enthusiasm has not escaped criticism. A further school of thought, to be discussed below, rejects the entire notion of cultural deprivation, but even some sociologists who broadly accept the analysis have expressed doubts as to the effectiveness of the proposed remedies. Advocates of community education and comparable initiatives claim no more than 'promising' past results. Sceptics prefer to say that the recorded improvements in children's performances have been no more than marginal. As already explained, a precise assessment of the impact of educational change has to wait at least until a generation has passed through the schools, but there are already substantial grounds for doubting whether the kind of innovations inspired by the Plowden Report can succeed.

Acland has identified a number of obstacles.[29] Firstly he points out that low-achieving pupils are not concentrated in a limited number of districts to the extent that would allow discrimination in favour of selected priority areas to reach more than a minority of disadvantaged children. Secondly he draws attention to evidence from the Plowden Committee's own research, showing how little of the variation in attainment amongst schoolchildren is explicable in terms of school variables, implying that simply injecting resources into Educational Priority Area schools will have little impact. Thirdly Acland questions whether parental attitudes can be divorced from their context and changed. Attitudes rather than material circumstances might exercise the most powerful direct influence upon children's progress at school, but the attitudes themselves could be rooted in material circumstances.

Following research amongst fifty-six inner-city families, Wilson and Herbert[30] argue that a culture that appears deprived from the point of view of the school is often an effective adjustment to circumstance. Aggression and physical toughness may be undesirable traits in the classroom, but they can help kids survive in streets where it is necessary for every individual to 'stick up for himself'. Given the circumstances to which they are a response, are working class parents' attitudes likely to change in response to a series of open days? A reluctance to 'interfere' and expecting that they will attend school to see the head-teacher only in the event of 'trouble' are related to working class parents' own experiences of education – in most cases experiences of failure. Evidence from America suggests that changing parental attitudes is an expensive process. A sustained improvement can require intensive case-work with parents through home visits extending over a period of years. Acland estimates the cost at £170 per year per child at 1972 prices. This goes well beyond the scale of positive discrimination that the Plowden Committee envisaged.

Although the project is reported enthusiastically, Young and McGeeney's action research indicates how difficult it can be to involve working class parents in their children's schooling.[31] Seventy-five per cent of the parents attended individually arranged talks with the class teachers, but only 44 per cent of the children had a parent who attended the exhibition of work and public talks given by the head and librarian, and only 15 per cent attended a discussion on teaching methods. A survey of parents found that most were satisfied with the school and their children's attainments. The main complaints concerned lax discipline and too much play. Expectations were modest and easily satisfied. One of the reasons why the problem of working class under-achievement persists is that the majority of working class parents are not conscious of any problem. Young and McGeeney encountered comparable difficulty in persuading the teachers of a problem whose solution required their active cooperation. It is a misconception to regard the teaching force as would-be missionaries awaiting a lead to raise working class levels of attainment. Despite the head's support for their project's aims, Young and McGeeney found that many teachers resented encroachment into their free time, and only three could be persuaded to visit pupils' homes.

Language

One version of the argument that sees working class culture militating against educational success focuses on the role of language, and this topic has attracted sufficient attention to merit separate discussion. The debate about the significance of language has been inspired mainly by Basil Bernstein's distinction between the public language or restricted code which he associates with working class culture, and the formal language or elaborated code which is alleged to be most common amongst the middle classes.[32] A difficulty in discussing Bernstein is that his ideas have earned a wide enough audience to have undergone extensive popularization and have been often vulgarized in the process. One writer tells us that, 'It seems above all to be a matter of command of language. Children from the lower classes learn fewer words, cannot express themselves as well, and this causes the development of their intelligence to lag behind. . . . In the first school years possible arrears must be made up as well as possible. This applies very strongly to countries like Britain, where a person's accent is enough to bring him or her social downgrading. The schools, or specialized teachers in them, ought to be able to make children with a "common" accent bi-lingual; young people ought to be given the freedom to speak their own Cockney but, if desired, to master an Oxford accent too.'[33] Although his name is frequently invoked to support this kind of assertion, Bernstein is really not guilty. Bernstein's work on language strikes so many chords that readers sometimes see unintended meanings. Most people are aware that working class speech is 'different'; that kids use slang and 'incorrect' accents, and that the vocabulary is narrow. It is easy to misread Bernstein as confirming popular hunches that these 'improper' uses of language must interfere with children's educational progress. In fact Bernstein's arguments are more sophisticated.

The term 'restricted code' refers principally to the syntax rather than the range or propriety of a vocabulary. In a restricted code syntax is rigid, speech condensed and words have definite meanings. Dialogue is punctuated into short sentences and commands, little use is made of adjectives, adverbs and impersonal pronouns, whilst considerable use is made of phrases such as 'Just fancy' and 'You know', whose function is to evoke a 'sympathetic circularity'. Reasons and conclusions tend to be left implicit. Bernstein's theory is not *only* about language. The importance of Bernstein's work lies in the correspondence he postulates between linguistic styles and, on the one hand, how individuals think, then on the other, how they communicate, attempt to influence and relate to each other. When persons are limited to a restricted code, Bernstein argues that constructing new concepts and adopting new ways of thinking become difficult, and that long-term goals are difficult to grasp. Communication with teachers and adjustment to school are hindered, and not only because children limited to a restricted code talk differently. In addition to this obvious problem, the children find it hard to understand the new situations, subjects and relationships encountered in school, together with the longer-term implications and purposes of education. Within a restricted code learning tends to be mechanical or, to use Klein's phrase, arbitrary.[34] Odd facts and ideas are digested but without real comprehension. Syntax involves definite rules (of grammar) of which individuals are rarely fully conscious, but which, in Bernstein's view, they use to develop and express their own ideas, and to de-code messages from others. Consequently, if individuals acquire only a restricted linguistic style, their coding apparatuses and their entire capacities for thought are similarly limited.

Bernstein argues that restricted codes evolve in milieux where personal relationships are clearly defined, particularly where they are backed with the force of tradition – circumstances typically present in long-established working class communities. In such situations, where everyone knows who's who, a restricted code can be an adequate medium for communication, often enriched by gestures and oral inflections endowed with traditional meanings. Bernstein does not claim that restricted codes are confined to the working class. In families and amongst close friends this type of speech is extremely common. He does claim, however, that in some sections of the working class children acquire no other linguistic style. Bernstein regards middle class work and community milieux as typically fluid, giving participants a sense of individuality. Communication requires an elaborated code with a flexible syntax which allows individuals to give precise expression to their own feelings and thoughts. This is also required in (typically middle class) families where what is expected of a child develops progressively with age, and where the child is expected to display autonomy and accept responsibility for his actions. Bernstein postulates a correspondence between social relationships, linguistic styles and how individuals think, with the language acting as the mediating factor. Children who have acquired an elaborated code are capable of what Klein terms problem-solving learning in which reasons are understood and separated from conclusions. New social relationships, subjects and meanings (including the meaning of school) are readily grasped. Hence the middle class child not only talks similarly to his teacher, but is equipped in a broader sense to slide smoothly into, and hence upwards through, the educational system. Bernstein's theory is not so much an alternative to other work on social class values and education, as a way of understanding the processes linking children's home backgrounds with their performances in school.

The research that Bernstein has directed makes it clear that the focal interest in language is an opening towards a fuller understanding of the ways in which patterns of family life and socialization are related to social class with implications for children's education. This research has been based upon 18 London primary schools, 13 in predominantly working class districts and 5 in mainly middle class areas. Samples of children have been subjected to batteries of tests, and their mothers interviewed before and two years after their children's entry into school. This enquiry has not only confirmed that the working and middle classes do tend to rely upon different linguistic styles, but that these differences are associated with the purposes for which language is used. Working class mothers stress the importance of language to transmit elementary skills, whereas middle class mothers emphasize its value when socializing children into inter-personal relationships.[35] In addition, when children 'pester' parents with questions, middle class mothers with their elaborated code are the more likely to actually answer rather than fend off the questions, to give full and correct answers, and to use compound arguments and analogies.[36] These middle class uses of language are themselves related to more general methods of controlling children. In working class households where the linguistic style is restricted, control tends to be 'imperative'; rules are laid down and enforced with punishments. Within Bernstein's sample it was possible to distinguish a different type of 'positional' control where rules were explicitly justified in terms, for example, of a child's age and sex – his position in the family. An even sharper contrast with the imperative style occurred where the control was 'personal', with rules justified in terms of the individual child's needs and personal qualities. This control was associated with the use of an elaborated code in middle class households.[37]

Other contrasts between middle and working class parenthood are rendered comprehensible when contextualized against the above findings. For example, the working class mothers in Bernstein's study tended to see the value of toys in terms of freeing parents from children's demands, whereas middle class mothers stressed toys' educational value.[38] Whilst 71 per cent of the middle class mothers claimed to read to their children frequently prior to school entry, only 19 per cent of the working class mothers did so. Working class mothers saw the task of preparing a child for school mainly in terms of giving instructions to behave, whereas middle class mothers sought to prepare their children to play more active roles in the classroom.[39] Given such contrasting experiences at home, it is easy to understand the research's finding that the middle class children entered school sharing teachers' ideas on rules of appropriate conduct, and consequently their classroom behaviour tended to be self-regulated, whereas the working class children had to learn from their schools what counted as acceptable conduct and their behaviour was typically teacher-regulated.[40]

This analysis of the working class child's difficulties has led to proposals for educational action paralleling those reviewed earlier, but with less emphasis on changing parents and a stress on the need to enrich beginning schoolchildren's language skills. Lawton, whose book on *Social Class, Language and Education*[41] broadly supports Bernstein's ideas, argues this case, whilst an action project, monitored by D. M. and G. A. Gahagan as part of Bernstein's own research, illustrates how this can be achieved.[42] The Gahagans describe how, in three mainly working class schools, a programme was introduced encouraging the children to ask questions, to expand upon their initial queries and to verbally explain the things they had done outside school. Bernstein has objected to working class children being labelled 'linguistically deprived' on the ground that their restricted codes are adequate foundations upon which the schools can build. He also rejects the concept of 'compensatory education' as ideologically loaded and implying that the schools are blameless for any eventual shortcomings in the children's attainments. Bernstein argues that no 'compensation' is required; only a proper education that takes as its starting point what working class pupils have to offer. But whilst rejecting the vocabulary of deprivation and compensation, Bernstein acknowledges a need for schools to supply working class children with linguistic and related cognitive skills that middle class children acquire at home.

Like most theories in sociology, Bernstein's ideas have encountered opposition. Rosen[43] queries whether the working and middle classes really employ such contrasting restricted and elaborated codes, and Edwards' research in two schools in North-west England failed to uncover large and consistent speech differences between pupils from different social class backgrounds.[44] Real life contrasts are less sharp than the restricted and elaborated concepts seem to imply, but Bernstein never claims that all manual families employ one code, and the remainder of the population a completely different one. The claim is rather that reliance upon a restricted code increases as the social hierachy is descended. Bernstein's own evidence confirms this proposition, and the enquiries of Lawton,[45] Heber[46] and Wootton[47] have offered independent support.

A different criticism, also voiced by Rosen, argues that even if middle and working class linguistic styles do differ, it need not follow that the former is superior in educational potential. Working class speech may differ from styles of expression commended in schools, but Rosen insists that it contains a rich capacity for expressing individual meanings, and on this point critiques of Bernstein interface with an alternative approach to explaining working class children's disadvantages.

Education as the problem

We are accustomed to asking why working class *children fail*. An alternative is to ask why the *schools fail* with working class children. In this latter approach, education rather than the working class child's presenting culture is seen as the likely source of his disadvantages. Since the late 1960s a 'new sociology of education' has appeared offering an 'alternative paradigm' which insists on *making* rather than simply *taking* and attempting to answer educational problems.[48] In education working class children are regarded as a problem; they are relatively difficult to teach and control. Conventional educational sociology has taken this problem and endeavoured to solve it. Investigators have sought to discover exactly what it is about the working class child and his background that militates against educational success. In this research, education itself along with its definitions of success is taken as given. In contrast, the new sociology of education regards education as problematic. Why are certain types of knowledge and attainment defined as educationally legitimate? Asking these questions has cast working class under-achievement in a new light.

Several complementary arguments have been developed within this new perspective. Firstly it is claimed, mainly by David Byrne and his associates, that the distribution of educational resources favours the middle classes, and rather than working class culture, it is working class education that is impoverished.[49] Data from local education authorities in England and Wales revealed a relationship between attainment levels and generosity of provision measured, for example, in terms of expenditure per pupil. Furthermore, provision was more generous in middle class areas. Hence the conclusion that 'differences in attainment are best explained as the outcome of class differences in political and economic power',[50] and that 'inequalities in school systems mirror and contribute to the maintenance of the general structure of inequality'.[51]

There are several difficulties with this argument. To begin with, could it account for the entire scale of working class under-achievement? How could it explain social class differences in attainment within schools? Secondly, in so far as levels of attainment and provision are related, the direction of casuality is unclear. Pupil success may not result from but cause resources to be allocated for examination work, sixth forms and higher education. Thirdly, the correlations between areas' social class compositions and levels of provision are far from perfect, and one critic has questioned whether the data collected by Byrne and his colleagues really support the conclusions they seek to draw.[52] It is not so much Byrne's evidence that is new as the method of analysis. Researchers usually proceed by accounting for variations in attainment in terms of pupil character-istics, leaving a residue to be explained in terms of school and education system factors which are then seen as playing secondary roles. This procedure is normally preferred because pupil factors such as measured intelligence and social class background can account for the greater proportion of the variance in attainment. Byrne insists on treating social class variables as operating, in the first instance, through their effects on types and levels of educational provision. The grounds for this insistence are dubious in view of the evidence that there is a greater variation in attainment between pupils from different social classes with provision held constant, than between populations of similar social class composition when provision varies.[53] Despite the higher levels of expenditure, the attainments of pupils in independent schools differ little from their social class peers in local authority systems.[54]

A second and more widely argued theme in the 'education as the problem' viewpoint asserts that education is so pervaded by middle class values as to inevitably favour children from middle class homes. It is claimed that working class values are different but not deficient – that they appear so only in a middle class educational system. Having discovered the 'culturally deprived child' in the 1960s, a great deal of subsequent sociological effort has been devoted to discrediting the concept. This argument begins with an analysis of education's ideological role. In a volume on *Schooling and Capitalism* we are told that 'Schooling is not just one among many of the social institutions which contribute to the perpetuation of the capitalist mode of production, it is arguably the most important'.[55] In one of the contributions to this volume Johnson discusses how mass schooling originally developed in nineteenth-century Britain as a process of class cultural control.[56] The concern of the authorities was not so much with vocational training or literacy as a broader moral mission. Industrialism required a type of education to instil children with qualities consistent with the factory system. The desired education was not available in private or dame schools, but needed a regimented public school where children acquired discipline under the ethos of the church. If this is the societal role of mass education, to prepare working class children for working class adulthoods, it is hardly surprising that few succeed in becoming upwardly mobile. Both society and education have changed since the nineteenth century, though it is arguable that the old elementary tradition lingers on in some working class primary schools, secondary moderns, and in the lower streams of some comprehensives. Since the nineteenth century, however, an educational 'ladder' has been instituted which is supposed to offer equal access to educational success. Yet despite changes in the officially declared purposes, it can be argued that education remains riddled with distinctly middle class values. In the alternative paradigm, education is treated as an imposition of meaning which occurs through the explicit curriculum and also through a hidden curriculum composed of teacher attitudes, the social organization of schools and classrooms, and the selection process. Meanings invariably carry an ideological loading and, it is alleged, continue to reflect the values of superordinate strata. School subjects such as English literature are unlikely to reflect interests nurtured in working class homes. Working class speech is labelled as inferior by both teachers and the 'research establishment'. The individual achievement towards which middle class careers are oriented operates as the model of educational success. Exposing working class children to this education has ideological implications. They mostly fail, but in the process can become convinced that this is due to their own lack of talent. It is argued that intelligence tests and other apparatuses of selection which seem to give all children a fair chance are really ideological devices which legitimize the privileges that the middle classes appear to earn.[57]

Writers who accept this analysis insist that working class culture is not incompatible with educability, and that all values, logics and speech styles are valid in their own terms. Labels such as 'deprived' can be employed only by imposing the values of an alien culture. Labov argues that whilst the non-standard English used by American blacks might be labelled as restricted and deficient in the schools, it is nevertheless capable of sustaining a logic which allows complex ideas to be developed and understood.[58] There is now a literature applauding the strengths of the inner-city child, such as his ability to 'get by' and cooperate with peers.[59] Keddie argues the feasibility of schools embodying working class values.[60] In her research into fourth-form teaching in a comprehensive school, Keddie found that working class pupils' apparent ineducability arose partly from an inability or unwillingness to accept their teachers' different definitions of the issues covered in a social studies course.[61] If teachers used working class English, offered subjects related to working class interests and organized schools in accordance with working class values by emphasizing, for example, collective as opposed to individual achievement, the working class child's handicaps might be transformed into assets.

It is necessary to bear in mind that no one has yet implemented an educational programme so closely attuned to working class values that the children's levels of attainment rivalled the middle class'. Is the entire curriculum valid only in relation to middle class values? Pupils from non-manual families might feel more at ease with their middle class teachers, but Lawton argues that certain forms of knowledge, as in science and mathematics, possess an objective validity.[62] He warns against exaggerating the contrasts between middle and working class cultures. Education that harmonises with middle class values need not alienate working class pupils. Furthermore, in so far as working class culture is different, it is difficult to see how some of its characteristics including the restricted code as described by Bernstein, and the subdued aspirations of parents could have other than disadvantageous implications in any educational system.

A third argument developed by those who regard 'education as the problem' concerns the self-fulfilling prophecy. Children tend to perform according to what is expected of them. In a widely reported enquiry, Rosenthal and Jacobson demonstrated that children whose teachers were told to expect substantial gains actually did improve their IQ scores, although these and a control group had been allocated to their classes at random.[63] Pidgeon has collated the results of studies in a number of countries showing that pupils' performances are conditioned by the expectations to which they are exposed as a result of their allocation to particular streams and different types of schools.[64] In Britain, Douglas has documented how primary schoolchildren's IQ scores improve or deteriorate depending on whether they are allocated to 'A' or 'C' streams.[65] Lacey[66] and Hargreaves,[67] in their respective studies of a grammar school and a secondary modern, have shown how an anti-academic subculture in which effort is directed away from the pursuit of scholastic success results from labelling pupils as failures by placing them in non-academic streams. There is some evidence that self-fulfilling prophecies work to the net disadvantage of working class pupils. In primary schools working class children are allocated to lower streams with greater frequency than would be predicted solely from their measured abilities.[68] Goodacre's research suggests that teachers regard a working class background as a handicap and align their expectations accordingly.[69] In her provocative case study, Keddie shows that even teachers who when discussing 'education' recognize the existence of working class potential that the schools fail to tap, adopt different attitudes in 'teaching' situations and treat working class pupils as unmotivated.[70] Keddie studied the actual execution of an humanities programme in which it was intended to offer an undifferentiated curriculum to all the fourth formers in a London comprehensive school, and found that teacher attitudes resulted in considerable differentiation at classroom level.

This argument probably contains some validity, but how much? It is naive to imagine that all pupils from working class homes are therefore labelled as unpromising. As Murphy points out, teachers do not ordinarily categorise children according to their social class backgrounds.[71] It is more common for teachers to distinguish children according to their abilities and social behaviour. Furthermore, Murphy argues that within classrooms teachers become sufficiently familiar with their pupils to distinguish evidence of ability from acceptable social behaviour, making it unlikely that working class children will be regarded as possessing limited potential simply because they are noisier, dirtier or otherwise less well behaved than their middle class peers. In addition, Murphy argues that teachers' assessments of children are made tentatively and are subject to change, thereby muting the operation of self-fulfilling prophecies. Nash's research underlines the complexity of the relationships between pupils' social class backgrounds and teacher evaluations.[72] In the primary school classrooms that Nash examined, teachers' evaluations of pupils were clearly related to the teachers' perceptions of the children's social class origins, but not to their *actual* class backgrounds. In some cases, the teachers were inferring class origins from pupil performance rather than basing their expectations upon a knowledge of the children's home circumstances.

The mosaic of educational inequality

If we have learnt anything since 1944 it must include the futility of debating working class under-achievement as if any one theory was likely to contain the whole answer. The truth is that educational success is affected by a host of factors many of which are related to social class. There is no one obstacle impeding working class children, but a mosaic of interacting processes. There is the unequal distribution of ability, innate or nurtured, parents who support, stimulate and encourage their children to varying extents, the linguistic and cognitive skills with which children enter school, opportunities in some areas and schools are relatively impoverished, whilst the values embedded in some teachers and teaching dampen rather than develop children's potential. Remedies addressed to any one source of inequality are liable to be smothered by the other countervailing processes.

If reformers' zeal could fire all cylinders simultaneously thereby loosening the relationship between children's life-chances and their social origins, it is naive to imagine that the result would be universally applauded. With the distribution of life-chances we are dealing in zero-sum equations. The opportunities available for some groups can be enlarged only by narrowing others. More upward mobility from the working class must mean more downward mobility from the middle classes. If it was only a matter of persuading people to vote for the principle, equality of opportunity would have arrived long ago. In absolute terms, working class educational standards have improved over recent generations. The longer-term life-chances of working class pupils have not improved commensurately because levels of attainment amongst the middle classes have also risen, keeping them as far ahead as ever. Raising general educational standards stimulates middle class parents to set their aspirations and encourage their children to still higher levels. How could this be prevented? We can be sure that measures to restrict middle class educational opportunities and increase the rate of downward mobility would encounter opposition.

Could support for such measures amongst the working class majority carry the argument? This is doubtful. In terms of educational attainment, the population is not tidily split into a uniformly successful middle class and a working class of failures. Levels of attainment gradually increase alongside other indices of socio-economic status. Within the working class, attainments gradually improve as one ascends the hierarchy from unskilled to skilled occupations. Likewise within the white-collar strata, average levels of attainment improve at each step up the job hierarchy. The pattern of educational inequality does not correspond to the dichotomous contours that split the population according to their subjective class identities and political affiliations. Educational achievement gradually increases alongside other types of privilege because the intervening variables upon which success at school directly depends are distributed in a similar manner. Average measured intelligence declines in a series of small steps between levels in the job hierarchy. Similarly the likelihood of parents visiting their children's schools, and their levels of aspiration gradually increase from the unskilled manual strata upwards. Bernstein's concepts of restricted and elaborated codes might appear to imply that individuals use either one or the other. In fact Bernstein's research shows that families' reliance on the elaborated and restricted codes together with their associated modes of control and socialization vary along a continuum,

Some of the ideal typical concepts used in discussions of the social class–educational achievement relationship imply misleadingly exaggerated contrasts. For example, Michael Lane discusses how, as a result of their different income careers, manual and non-manual families develop dissimilar 'models of the world'.[73] White-collar careers tend to be secure and progressive, leading to broader ideas about the nature of society incorporating these features. Blue-collar careers, in contrast, are uncertain and fluctuating, resulting in perceptions of the world as an unstable and unpredictable place in which investing effort in education to achieve long-term rewards appears scarcely rational. This kind of contrast can be useful provided we remember that we are talking in terms of ideal types – exaggerations of tendencies that vary in their prominence between the middle and working classes. In reality working and middle class attitudes are less opposed than Lane's concepts suggest. Research in both America and Britain shows that in relation to their own educational and occupational experience, working class parents are the *more* ambitious for their children.[74] In absolute terms working class aspirations are lower than middle class parents', but this does not reflect a disinterest in self-advancement; it is a consequence of starting from a lower rung on the ladder. Working class parents are neither disinterested in education nor unconcerned that their children should 'get on'. During his journey into the working class, Leighton discovered that, 'Though Charlie [a roadsweeper] had a working man's contempt for theory against practice, he most bitterly regretted his education had been cut short, and was determined that his family would have a better start. They were his pride: a son who was a junior officer in the merchant marine, an elder daughter who was a secretary in a government department.'[75] These modest achievements would arouse little pride amongst the professional classes, but from a working class start things look different. Obtaining an apprenticeship following CSE or O-levels is success for the son of an unskilled worker.

For working class pupils, school and home are less likely to be mutually supportive than amongst the middle classes, but this should not lead us to imagine that working class pupils are typically perplexed and discontented. Witkin's study of over 3,000 fourth formers found no consistent relationship between positive evaluations of school and social class,[76] and his working class sample actually recorded the most positive evaluations of English lessons. The main social class difference that Witkin uncovered was that the middle class pupils possessed the more strongly articulated superordinate expectations, meaning that they evaluated their schooling in terms of larger objectives such as university entry. These expectations made them more capable of recognizing and responding to educational opportunities, and also encouraged them to be critical of what individual teachers offered.

The mosaic of class-related variables that generate unequal opportunity are distributed throughout the population in such intricate patterns that it is difficult to envisage the social engineering that would make individuals' life-chances independent of their social origins. This would not merely require, for example, enriching working class children's linguistic skills, but applying the enrichment unevenly within both the working and middle classes in reverse proportions to the linguistic advantages otherwise liable to be conferred by different home backgrounds. Inequalities between ethnic groups are easier to address. If only a few members of such a group take a few steps up the class structure, with the next generation these gains are there to build on, and it is possible for the group to spread into all levels of society step-by-step. Social class inequalities are different. The working class child is always going to be starting from near the foot of the hierarchy. Maybe we should heed Jencks' advice:[77] cease trying to use education to redistribute life-chances, and judge types of schooling in terms of their intrinsic satisfactions. Boudon argues that the most effective route towards redressing inequalities of opportunity would be through compressing other socio-economic inequalities.[78] A reduction in general social class differences would yield exponential gains by narrowing the class differential at each educational hurdle. The social class–educational achievement relationship may be a fact of life that we simply have to accept unless other social and economic inequalities can be tempered.

Power, politics and ideology 6

The nature of power

Noting its majority enrolment in trade unions and support for the Labour Party starts rather than concludes a discussion of working class politics. Power is a complex phenomenon. Unlike resources such as motor cars and houses we cannot directly observe it. Rather than a 'thing', power is better regarded as an attribute of social relationships; the ability of a person or group to have others do things they would not otherwise have done. This ability reflects the resources (ranging from money and guns to ideas) available to different groups; resources which can be used to alter the perceived costs and benefits with which others' behaviour can be sanctioned. Power is not so much another type of inequality as a corollary of the unequal distribution of other resources. It is a consequence of other inequalities in so far, for example, as wealth can be used to control others. Simultaneously it can be the source of inequalities as when powerful groups influence others in order to add to their stock of wealth. Power has been likened to a metaphor.[1] We cannot measure it directly and must infer its distribution from its sources and consequences.

Oppression need not accompany power. 'Power over', when one group asserts itself at the expense of others, is an inappropriate description of some power relationships. There is also 'power with' which occurs when resources are mobilized to achieve collective ends. For example, the community concentrates power in the hands of teachers so that children may be educated. Likewise the courts are given powers that enable the laws of the land to be upheld. However, in a society where different sections of the community possess different interests and aspirations, power inevitably entails dominant and subordinate groups.

Ideas are amongst the resources generating power, for when groups with other assets can propagate beliefs justifying their positions, naked power is transformed into legitimate authority and thereby magnified. Legitimacy consolidates and stabilizes power relationships, and also complicates their analysis. In his essay on power, Lukes criticizes and argues a need to look beyond the one-dimensional view that regards power *merely* as the ability to get others to do things they would not otherwise have done.[2] The ability of powerful groups to manipulate ideas means that subordinates may never become conscious of some possible courses of action. Issues may never be placed on the 'agenda' for public debate. Even more insidiously, ideological power may be used to influence other groups' conscious preferences. This type of ideological dominance is known as hegemony.

Under the more extreme forms of slavery as practised in America's South, power relationships were easy to discern. The masters enjoyed virtually absolute power. The slaves possessed no property or weapons, they were not free to organize amongst themselves, nor to express beliefs inconsistent with their status. Why did the slaves acquiesce, as so many did for so long? Had they any alternative? With the working class in contemporary society the situation is more complicated. Workers do not own the means of production and are second class citizens at work, not only in terms of remuneration but in a host of additional ways. They cannot afford the life-styles that are visibly enjoyed by more privileged strata, and the odds are against either their children or themselves rising out of the working class. The term wage-slavery is sometimes used, but the working class is obviously not oppressed as were the American slaves. Workers are free to organize in families, community groups, trade unions and political parties. All adults have the vote, and its numerical strength means that the working class has control over government at its fingertips. Through their trade unions workers are capable of generating considerable power when disposed to flex their muscles. So why is the working class still a lower class? It is easy to talk of a dominance of conservative values emanating from privileged strata, but the situation is clearly not so straightforward. The working class is not meekly acquiescent. It has organized itself in trade unions and lent support to a Labour Party purportedly committed to social changes to redistribute privilege. Spokesmen for capital complain of a hegemony of socialist values which make profit a dirty word.

Marx's theories continue to haunt sociological debate. The working class in Britain has not united into a revolutionary force, but sociologists have never lost sight of the reasons why it might do so. Debate about its political role has therefore pivoted around the problem as to why the working class has failed to develop the type of consciousness that would precipitate revolutionary change – why working class organizations have not transformed society, and an array of answers has been offered.

This chapter groups these answers under four headings, but fitting the literature into these boxes has required some vigorous massage. As will become evident, there are numerous points of dispute between writers grouped under particular headings, and considerable overlap between the schools of thought. The headings serve as signposts through a complex literature and enable some principal lines of controversy to be illuminated, but it is not assumed that the arguments contained beneath any one heading will enjoy a monopoly of truth. Indeed, the overall argument to be developed insists that a complete understanding of the position of the working class in the power structure requires an imaginative combination of the various contributions.

Immediate milieux

The first answer points out that few manual workers are sociologists and tend not to see their society from the peculiar detached position that the sociologist endeavours to assume. This need not mean that workers are guilty of false consciousness; that their beliefs are wrong. Just as the appearance of a building varies when perceived from different angles, so societies appear differently when viewed from the many positions they contain. Individuals do not ordinarily see their society as would an impartial observer. They witness their society's practices including its inequalities from various egocentric positions, and the resultant images of society that are formed in its members' minds may be no less valid than the sociologist's, but simply different.

This argument was initially applied to class analysis by Elizabeth Bott whose research was designed primarily to investigate family life.[3] Bott was interested in the differences between families where the roles of husband and wife were segregated, the man's life centred on work and mates whilst the woman's world hinged around home and family, and where the conjugal roles were joint with greater sharing and similarity in the lives of the partners. To explore these contrasting styles of family life, Bott interviewed a haphazardly assembled sample of twenty households. Such research may prove little yet be rich with insights, which Bott's study certainly was. Indeed, it ranks as one of the most influential enquiries in the history of British sociology. On the basis of her evidence Bott hypothesized that relationships between husbands and wives vary depending upon the types of social networks by which the partners are surrounded. Firstly she distinguished closed networks, illustrated in longer-established working class communities, where circles of kin, neighbours and work-mates are superimposed, meaning that they are composed of the same persons, and argued that in this type of context husbands and wives tend to retain their own associates after marriage, resulting in segregated roles. Secondly she distinguished open networks, characteristic amongst the middle classes where kin, neighbours and work associates tend to be different persons, resulting in networks of linked rather than superimposed circles. This type of network appeared to encourage emotional dependence and closeness in marriage. Largely as a by-product of her interest in styles of marriage, Bott discovered that these networks were associated with different 'class ideologies', suggesting that individuals form conceptions of their wider society by amplifying the social relationships in which they are immediately involved. The closed network was related to a 'power model' in which society was seen as composed of 'us', usually the working class, and 'them'. Superimposing kin, work-place and other relationships resulted in a strong sense of community in which individuals experienced a sharp distinction between their own kind and other groups. In contrast, the open network seemed to nurture a 'prestige hierarchy' model in which individuals were aware of minute variations in prestige between a large number of positions. Orientations towards the occupants of higher positions tended to be emulative, the total image of society resembling a ladder inviting individuals to climb, whereas the power model militated against any desire to join the 'other side'.

In an article written in conjunction with *The Affluent Worker* David Lockwood[4] extended Bott's typology of class ideologies. Lockwood accepted Bott's major theoretical premise, that individuals' images of society depend not so much upon the shape of the overall social structure, but upon the primary social relationships in which they are directly involved. He argued, however, that it was possible to distinguish three types of working class milieux each giving rise to its own image of society. Firstly, Lockwood discussed the proletarian worker, whose circumstances were similar to the closed networks that Bott identified. These circumstances, according to Lockwood, are found in industries such as shipbuilding, coal-mining and dockwork where large numbers of workers doing similar jobs live and work in mutual dependence but in substantial isolation from the wider society. The result, according to this theory, is a comradeship which encourages an us–them image of society and underwrites 'solidaristic' support for working class institutions including trade unions and the Labour Party. Lockwood argued that not all manual workers are located in proletarian situations. He also distinguished deferential workers, purportedly found in agriculture and small-scale industry; milieux characterized by personal relations of dependence upon employers, and 'particularistic' local communities with individuals knowing each other as persons and attributing status on the basis of personal qualities. This type of milieu, according to Lockwood, results in every person knowing his rightful place and, rather than feeling antagonistic towards or modelling themselves upon superiors, individuals simply acknowledge the propriety of the hierarchy. The theme of *The Affluent Worker*[5] is that these traditional milieux are being replaced by a different working class setting. Lockwood argues that proletarian and deferential workers are 'found in industries and communities which, to an ever-increasing extent, are backwaters of national industrial and urban development'.[6] In places such as Luton it is claimed that a new privatized worker is appearing. Privatized workers are engaged upon specialized but routine jobs where the employee lacks autonomy, as on the car assembly-line. The result is low job involvement and an exceptionally instrumental approach towards work. The privatized worker tends to live in a mobile neighbourhood harbouring only weak primary group loyalties. Kin are dispersed and neighbourhood relationships undeveloped. These circumstances heighten privatization and reinforce instrumental as opposed to solidaristic attachments not only to work but to other institutions including trade unions and the Labour Party. The evidence from the Luton enquiry indicated that these circumstances encourage a pecuniary image of society, with individuals feeling that they belong amidst a large central mass of discrete persons and families amongst whom status is judged in terms of material possessions.

A feature of Lockwood's scheme is that none of the typified workers is class conscious in the Marxist sense. This has been a major criticism of the typology; that it allows no place for the socialist worker. Proletarian workers recognize a conflict of interest with 'them' and are prepared to act collectively in the interests of their own group. However, the 'us' in the us–them equation consists of the local work-group and community rather than a society-wide class.

Contrary to the presumption of some of *The Affluent Worker's* critics, the privatized worker is not necessarily acquiescent. Instrumental orientations do not guarantee that individuals' jobs will match their aspirations, as Goldthorpe has made clear in his discussion of industrial relations in contemporary Britain. When the Royal Commission on Trade Unions and Employers' Associations was deliberating in the 1960s, an influential body of opinion defined Britain's relations problem as follows.[7]

✅ It was noted that national negotiations between trade unions and employers were generally conducted in an orderly manner. Beneath this level, however, the post-war years had seen the emergence of a grass-roots trade union movement symbolized by the growing influence of shop stewards. Full employment together with the spread of piece-rates and bonus systems had created scope for wage-drift and workplace bargaining which was conducted in a characteristically disorderly manner. Shop stewards had no recognized place in the formal structures of many unions, and factory-level bargaining was rarely covered by agreed procedures. The perceived results were unofficial strikes, inflationary wage-drift and differentials running out of control, thereby causing widespread dissatisfaction. Fox and Flanders argued that the solution was to rationalize bargaining at the plant level so that order would replace the jungle. Goldthorpe[8] argued in reply that such measures would be insufficient. Integration, in Goldthorpe's view, required a general moral regulation on inequalities which plant-based bargaining, however orderly, could not supply. Differentials would remain a jungle until inequalities became governed by a generally accepted morality. Until such a morality was established, and Goldthorpe did not regard it as imminent, wage claims would continue to leap-frog and groups of workers would use whatever muscle they possessed to maximize their rewards.

Lockwood's typology allows for conflict and accounts for its different forms. Proletarian workers will take such action as appears necessary to protect and enhance the interests of the communities in which they are immersed. Amongst privatized sections of the labour force a condition of anomie tends to prevail in which aspirations and conduct are unregulated by any agreed norms. The typology, however, recognizes no circumstances that encourage a generalized working class consciousness and solidarity, and therefore offers an explanation as to why a revolutionary situation has not arisen. The answer is simply that there are no working class milieux that typically encourage the type of consciousness that would precipitate such a situation.

This typology has won considerable attention and equally justified criticism. An immediate point for debate concerns whether workers' images of society really do vary in the manner that the typology describes. When initially constructed the typology was an imaginative interpretation of the limited evidence then available, but subsequent research in Liverpool[9] has failed to discover variations in manual workers' images of society corresponding to the circumstances that Lockwood outlined, and other attempts to locate workers with the relevant images in their prescribed habitats have been equally unsuccessful. Brown's investigation amongst Wallsend shipbuilding workers,[10] and Moore's research into nineteenth-century Durham coal-mining villages[11] failed to uncover the emphatically proletarian attitudes that Lockwood's typology suggests should have arisen. Workers in agriculture[12] and small-scale manufacturing industry[13] have been investigated, but without discovering especially deferential types of imagery. Furthermore, as one member of the research team has subsequently disclosed,[14] the evidence in the Luton enquiry suggesting that privatized workers develop a distinctly pecuniary brand of imagery was ambiguous and susceptible to alternative interpretations. In his survey of the now available evidence, Moorhouse[15] concludes that rather than emphasizing the differences, it is more realistic to stress the features common to all working class images of society such as an awareness of belonging to a subordinate class, and a feeling that many privileges enjoyed by superordinate strata are unmerited.

A second criticism concerns the stress that Bott and Lockwood place upon the worker's immediate environment. Their theories portray workers as almost completely insensitive to the macro–scheme of inequality amidst which they live, and untouched by broader ideological currents. This is surely unrealistic. Moore's study of Durham pit villages[16] has indicated that, in the nineteenth century, the methodist religion was an important influence encouraging not only the miners, but also their trade union leaders to adopt an 'organismic' as opposed to a conflict view of industrial relations, whilst during the twentieth century the presence of a Labour Party broadcasting a socialist ideology has made a considerable impact in the villages. It might be foolish to dismiss as irrelevant the primary social relationships by which workers are surrounded, but it is doubtful whether they warrant the importance assigned in the work of Bott and Lockwood.

The institutionalization of conflict: the pluralist theory

The second explanation of the failure of the working class to develop into a revolutionary force follows a different track to talk about the institutionalization of conflict, how Britain has become a socially plural society containing multiple centres of power, and how gradual evolutionary change has removed the need for revolution. This argument notes that since the nineteenth century the working class has developed organizations, principally the trade unions and the Labour

Party, to enhance its own interests. Rather than leading to revolutionary confrontation, however, these developments are seen as having transformed Britain from a society dominated by a relatively monolithic establishment or ruling class, to a pluralist society in which numerous sections of the population organize themselves and thereby generate the power to represent their interests. Organizations representing different interests have become linked in bargaining and negotiating relationships. Rather than seeking to destroy the opposition they have sought compromises. Trade unions are recognized by managements and in politics the working class has been enfranchised. The result is that working class aspirations, amongst others, are gradually realized, and the end-product is sometimes called a post-capitalist society.

During the 1950s this thinking was developed in two influential books. In British politics Anthony Crosland's *The Future of Socialism*[17] argued that capitalism had already been transformed by previous Labour governments, the trade unions, and by a transfer of power from the owners of industry to salaried managers and technocrats. Crosland saw no reason why the gradual realization of working class interests should not continue, and these claims gave theoretical justification to 'revisionist' thinking in the Labour Party, the basic tenet of revisionism being that socialist thought must evolve to take account of an already accomplished transformation of society. Around the same time, in his work on *Class and Class Conflict in Industrial Society*, Ralph Dahrendorf[18] was presenting similar arguments to a sociological audience. Dahrendorf argued that class conflict had not disappeared and, therefore, that the Marxist theory of society stressing the reality of conflict remained relevant. At the same time, Dahrendorf argued that the orthodox Marxist scenario of class struggle eventually leading to revolution needed modification. He argued that class conflict had become institutionalized in both industry and politics, and thereby accommodated into the social system which was being changed in a peaceful, evolutionary manner.

Ross and Hartman's work on *Changing Patterns of Industrial Conflict*[19] applied these ideas to the industrial scene. A comparison of strike activity in a number of countries led Ross and Hartman to the

139

conclusion that recognition of trade unions by managements and the establishment of bargaining relationships together with working class political parties taking issues such as social security out of the industrial and into the political arena, tended to reduce disruptive conflict in industry. Over time, they argued, the trend was towards a diminishing incidence of strikes, and their book speculated about strikes eventually 'withering away'. In a recent assessment of the Ross and Hartman thesis, Ingham[20] has expressed doubts as to whether strikes can ever wither away world-wide to the extent that has occurred in especially favourable circumstances such as those present in Scandinavia, but does not challenge the possibility of conflict being accommodated within capitalist industry. Orthodox Marxists regard the interests of capital and labour as basically antagonistic and, in the final analysis, incapable of reconciliation. In contrast, the view embedded in the theories now under consideration is that class interests can be reconciled, maybe never with finality, but through a series of temporary truces. In their research on comparative politics, Rose and Urwin[21] have concluded that class interests are not the major threat to stability sometimes imagined because they *are* susceptible to bargaining and compromise. Political parties based upon working class support seek objectives such as improved pay levels, social security payments and educational opportunities; issues that always leave scope for compromise over, for example, the amount by which real wages should rise. In contrast, Rose and Urwin argue that it is parties based on religious or nationalist ideologies that tend to take entrenched stands on non-negotiable issues which pose a major threat to stability.

A substantial body of research has endorsed the view that the unions are better regarded as organizations for encapsulating and resolving disputes than waging a class war. The national enquiries conducted by the Government Social Survey have exploded the myth of strike-prone British industry suffering at the hands of militant shop stewards. In the mid-1960s it was found that the attitudes of both rank-and-file trade unionists and shop stewards were overwhelmingly non-militant, and that 66 per cent of all unionists had never experienced a strike in their present firms.[22] Another national enquiry in the early 1970s covering 198 different establishments found that 70 per cent of the managers talked about how shop stewards *helped* them to *solve* industrial relations' problems. Indeed, 46 per cent of the managers went on to note that the stewards were helpful in dealing with *production* difficulties. For their part, 89 per cent of the stewards reported that managers in their firms accepted them willingly.[23] Cousins' interviews with 42 shop stewards and 226 workers in Tyneside shipyards produced further evidence of non-militant orientations, *especially* amongst the stewards.[24] Rather than provoking trouble, the stewards were committed to procedural norms and resolving disputes through agreed channels. The influential 'Oxford School'[25] has consistently backed a liberal/pluralist view of industrial relations. Unitary conceptions of the enterprise have been opposed for assuming an unrealistic harmony of interests. Conflict is recognized as a fact of industrial life, but one which can be contained because of an ultimate mutual interest in the survival of the enterprise in which all groups of workers, managers and owners are involved. Hence the Oxford School's advocacy of voluntarism and collective bargaining as the most effective strategies in industrial relations.

In his illustration of *Marxist Sociology in Action*, J. A. Banks has restated the institutionalization of conflict theory.[26] Banks' ideas are inspired by his own research in the steel industry, the evidence from which is seen as requiring a considerable modification, though not the abandonment, of Marx's original theory. The modification is to argue that capitalism is gradually evolving towards a collectivist rather than a classless society. In steel as in other industries, Banks notes the development of trade unions which represent the workers' views to both managements and the state, but do not challenge the existence of either. Likewise Banks notes that the pressures the unions exerted through the Labour Party in favour of nationalizing the steel industry were consistently on the managerial grounds of enhancing efficiency rather than as a step towards workers' control. Banks argues that technological and organizational imperatives in industrial society mean that managerial hierarchies and the state cannot wither away. The actual 'revolutionary' significance of trade unions and their leaders, therefore, is to establish a collectivist role for themselves, a development that has already been largely accomplished.

Critics of this interpretation of the place of the working class in the power structure dwell upon two types of evidence. Firstly, it is argued that ostensibly working class organizations do not always reflect working class interests. A great deal of significance can be attached to the fact that whilst its voters are predominantly working class, at the Parliamentary level the Labour Party has become a middle class body. Guttsman has documented the process by which, as it has become a party of government, there has been a middle class influx into the Labour Party in Parliament.[27] In 1945–51 approximately a half of Labour cabinet ministers had personal histories in manual occupations, but since 1964 such characters have virtually disappeared from the front bench. Johnson has noted how similar in social composition the Conservative and Labour élites have become.[28] In the Conservative Party the traditional dynasties of Tory families, and politicians with gentry backgrounds have made way for members from business and the professions. Meanwhile in the Parliamentary Labour Party working class members have diminished to be replaced by university-educated and 'professional' politicians, that is, persons who make politics into a full-time and life-long career. Johnson also notes the emergence of family dynasties in the Labour Party; members of Parliament whose parents held high office in the labour movement. Hindess has shown that the decline of working class Labour politics has not been confined to the Parliamentary level.[29] His research in Liverpool found a strong middle class element at ward meetings. Though working class members were still in considerable evidence, it was the middle class members who emerged as candidates for the local council, and whilst the party machine remained vigorous in areas with a strong middle class membership, in working class districts the party was dying at the grass-roots.

Trade union leaders continue to be mostly drawn from the rank-and-file. University-educated, 'professional' officials account for little more than a trickle into research departments. Nevertheless, there is an argument which claims that, irrespective of their origins, the experience of office tends to dissociate trade union leaders from their members' interests. This argument was initially expounded by Robert Michels early in the century, and has subsequently undergone numerous restatements.[30] Michels proclaimed 'the iron law of oligarchy', insisting that however democratic an organization's initial ideals and constitution, once installed in office leaders are able to manipulate the rank-and-file. Occupying office gives leaders control over their organizations' finances and communication channels. They are entrusted to arrange agendas and can acquire reputations amongst their memberships. The experience of office gives incumbents skills and information that other members cannot match. What is more, Michels claimed that the life-styles of trade union officials (and leaders of working class political parties as well) acquire more in common with the middle classes than their own members. As a result, he argued, leaders tend to lose touch with the grass-roots. Simultaneously, they acquire vested interests in maintaining the organizations upon which their own jobs and life-styles depend. The organizations that were built as means to achieve particular goals become regarded as ends in themselves. Trade union officials come to regard collective bargaining, for example, as their movement's *raison d'être*, and begin to accommodate members' interests to the existing economic system instead of challenging it.

Needless to say, this view of trade union and Labour Party leaders as 'class traitors' is open to challenge. Supporters of the pluralist theory argue that the Labour Party membership selects middle class leaders because they happen to be the most effective representatives of working class interests. As regards the trade unions, Warner[31] has pointed to processes that can off-set the tendencies that Michels described. Trade unions are voluntary associations; members can drop-out or desert to other bodies. Leaders, therefore, must pay continuing attention to rank-and-file aspirations. Furthermore, despite the advantages that accrue to existing office-holders, trade union leaders can be toppled when, as is often the case, they are obliged to present themselves for periodic re-election. Warner argues that this electoral check preserves elements of uncertainty, unpredictability and populism in the trade union movement.

Opponents of the pluralist theory remain unimpressed by these arguments. Following a survey of élite groups across a range of political and business institutions, Guttsman argues that whilst its membership has widened, it remains realistic to talk of a ruling class in Britain.[32] In the nineteenth century national life was dominated by the land-owning strata. Subsequently the professional and business classes have made inroads, but working class representation remains weak. Guttsman talks about how the propertied classes continue to be strongly represented in key positions in politics, business and public administration, and how beliefs and values nurtured in this ruling class pervade key institutions. Likewise, the articles assembled in Wakeford and Urry's *Power in Britain*[33] disclose how upper middle class personnel in industry, finance and politics form an interlocking web, cemented through kinship and individuals who occupy multiple élite positions, to preserve power in the hands of the privileged.

A second strand of criticism against the pluralist theory focuses upon the proof of the pudding. To what extent has the alleged dispersion of power in favour of working class organizations led to a redistribution of privilege? Critics point to the general long-term stability of income differentials between occupational groups, and to the failure of the welfare state to effect a large-scale transfer of resources in favour of the working class.[34] And many attach great importance to how unequally private property remains distributed. According to the Royal Commission on the Distribution of Income and Wealth, in 1973 the wealthiest 10 per cent still owned 67.3 per cent of the nation's privately held assets.[35] The data assembled by Atkinson show how such redistribution that has occurred since early in the century has taken place mainly within the top 10 per cent; from the super-rich to the very rich.[36] In an analysis of data from sixty western and third world countries, Jackman has shown that, with levels of economic development held constant, political democracy has no significant effects upon social equality as measured either in terms of the distribution of income or the scale and shape of welfare provision.[37] From this evidence, it is not the fruits of working class power that are impressive so much as the success of privileged strata in conserving their advantages.

Once again, defenders of the pluralist position offer alternative interpretations of the evidence. As regards the distribution of wealth, Polanyi and Wood[38] claim that the figures which emphasise the persistence of steep inequalities mislead by refusing to include the more widely-held forms of property such as houses and motor cars in their calculations. These writers estimate that the top 10 per cent own 'only' 52 per cent of all personally held wealth. Furthermore, calculating trends in the distribution of private property ignores the redistribution that has occurred from private into public ownership. The egalitarian impact of the welfare state can also be emphasized or minimized depending upon the evidence that is presented. According to the Royal Commission's calculations, if the equivalent capital value of state pension rights is taken into account, the share of private wealth held by the bottom 80 per cent rises from 13.6 to 40.7 per cent. As regards the failure of wage-earners to benefit from a substantial redistribution of property incomes, the situation is simply that the proportion of the national income flowing to property is too small to make any great difference to working class standards of living; '. . . if three-quarters of what companies distributed to shareholders and proprietors in 1972 (not a bad year for profits) had been handed out in pay packets to the whole workforce, it would have increased real wages by only 9 per cent. That does not sound bad, but it would have been a once-for-all rise.'[39] The fact that few major changes have occurred in the positions of occupational groups in the national pay league can be interpreted as implying not that the entire working class remains oppressed, but that traditionally privileged groups of workers have succeeded in maintaining their advantages. Everyone favours the principle of helping the low-paid, but which trade unions advocate the erosion of their own members' differentials?

The incorporation of the working class

Until the late 1960s the immediate milieux argument and the institutionalization of conflict were favourite sociological explanations of working class acquiescence. They still enjoy some support, but more recently a substantial body of opinion has been convinced by the contrary evidence and argument, and an alternative theory has grown in popularity alleging the incorporation of the working class. This theory reassesses the significance of institutions that pluralists treat as articulating working class interests. Rather than having been fashioned by the working class to realize its own aspirations, it is argued that during their development the trade unions and the Labour Party were strongly influenced by superordinate interest groups. As a result, it is claimed that the real role of these institutions is to contain working class aspirations so as to avoid any serious challenge to vested interests, whilst creating an illusion of working class interests being served. The theory also maintains that conservative values fostering acquiescence in existing social arrangements are filtered from more privileged strata to inhibit the emergence of an authentic working class consciousness. The filtering is said to occur through education, the mass media, religion and political parties, and the net result is the incorporation of the working class into exploitive class relationships. Rather than indicating the *collectivism* that Banks alleges, this theory sees trade unions and other organizations that link the working class to centres of power as branches of a *corporatist* state.

Under a corporatist system state power is exercised not through a monolithic bureaucratic apparatus, but by the state 'licensing' apparently autonomous corporations to perform stipulated functions and endowing them with the necessary rights whilst they discharge their responsibilities. This status is particularly clear in the case of *QUAGOS*, quasi-governmental organisations such as the British Boardcasting Corporation and the National Enterprise Board which are established but not directly administered by the executive. The corporatist argument draws attention to the growth of *QUAGOS* and suggests that comparable relationships are being forged between governments and large-scale industry on the one hand, and the trade unions on the other. Free enterprise is permitted, but firms are expected to acknowledge governments' wishes as regards investment and pricing policies. Trade unions are granted freedom to organize and bargain, and may have their rights extended as under the 1974 Labour government's legislation which, amongst other provisions, legalized the close shop and required that shop stewards be granted time off work on full pay whilst discharging their duties. Whilst this legislation was being enacted, however, the trade unions were expected to develop and honour an understanding with the government – a social contract stipulating a ceiling on pay increases. The incorporation theory does not accept that workers' everyday circumstances make the growth of a generalized and radical consciousness unlikely. Nor does it accept that the working class is winning the class struggle in a gradual, evolutionary manner. The situation is seen as one in which the superordinate strata are, at least temporarily, holding their ground through a combination of organizational and ideological processes which defuse working class opposition.

These alternative interpretations of the power structure under discussion are associated with different political ideologies. Indeed, it is their ideological connotations that generate most of the passion by which the theories are surrounded. Pluralists almost invariably approve of the power structure that their theory purports to describe, whilst the incorporation theory is associated with a left-wing critique of existing socio-political arrangements. Sociologists' personal political convictions are always liable to influence their assessments of a theory. It is possible, in principle, to identify the facts that are in dispute, and subsequently measure the theories against the evidence rather than their political appeal. In practice, unfortunately, the facts at issue are often difficult to isolate for purely objective appraisal.

Following his studies of the nineteenth-century working class, Foster has argued that 'the changes associated with liberalisation (the extension of the vote, the development of mass parties, the legal recognition of trade unions) were quite obviously part of a process by which specifically capitalist authority was reimposed and the working class vanguard pushed back into isolation. Obviously, too, it was the earlier development of some form of mass class consciousness which originally made this necessary.'[40] Foster researched the industrial revolution and its immediate aftermath in Oldham, and discovered that the imposition of the factory system provoked widescale dissent. Socialist ideas were rife and at times the situation seemed pre-revolutionary. Neither Oldham nor any other single place could be claimed as the typical industrial town. Indeed, Foster's own research found few glimmerings of revolutionary working class consciousness in either nineteenth-century South Shields or Northampton. But he argues that the dissent uncovered in Oldham must also have been present elsewhere. Hence the nation-wide series of moves, from the mid-nineteenth century onwards, aimed at encapsulating working class opposition. These developments are conventionally construed as liberalization and, by pluralists, as resulting in a growth of working class power. Foster claims, however, that the 'emancipation' of the working class was carefully managed so as to actually consolidate capitalist authority. The key process, in Foster's view, was the creation of an aristocracy of labour consisting of relatively well-paid workers who, with the encouragement of employers, acquired a superior status and respectability, and subsequently became cemented into the social system through friendly societies, education and the temperance movements. The franchise was extended to the working class in stages with the more prosperous sections, the aristocracy of labour, in the forefront, and likewise the first trade unions to be recognized represented the skilled workers. Foster argues that this process of liberalization was consciously manipulated to produce a labour movement with a leadership that aligned itself with bourgeois interests. The effect, in the nineteenth century, was to fragment the working class and to leave its class conscious, socialist elements as an isolated group.

In his analysis of the political incorporation of the working class, Moorhouse argues along essentially similar lines that the manner in which liberalization proceeded had consequences reaching down to the present day.[41] Moorhouse shows that, prior to 1918, there were severe structural constraints on working class political opposition. Voter registration technicalities, the financial costs of political activity and the bias of the electoral system against urban areas all inhibited the development of working class politics despite the extension of the franchise to the majority of manual workers during the second half of the nineteenth century. It was not until 1918 that the entire working class achieved the vote. The relatively prosperous and respectable strata were enfranchised earlier, and the obstacles to effective political organization encouraged alliances with bourgeois interests. Moorhouse argues that during this period a pragmatic deference became institutionalized as the dominant style of working class politics in Britain, and that this style has remained dominant ever since. Jessop endorses this analysis,[42] insisting that the deference and civility that others[43] have considered just part of Britain's political culture can be subsumed under class analysis. In his historical study of the working class in Edinburgh, Gray confirms the significance of the aristocracy of labour.[44] Such an aristocracy could be discerned in nineteenth-century Edinburgh. It consisted of skilled workers including the engineers who developed a distinctive life-style made possible by superior levels of pay and stability of employment. In Edinburgh, as Foster and Moorhouse argue happened on a national scale, this labour aristocracy played a key role in the creation of a reformist-oriented labour movement within which working class politics were subsequently contained.

According to this theory, the incorporation of the working class on terms unfavourable to itself is not maintained without constant attention, principally of an ideological nature. The apparent representation of their interests through trade unions and the Labour Party encourages workers to acquiesce under existing socio-economic arrangements. Although it is not actually delivered, the educational system creates an appearance of equal opportunity, whilst the mass media broadcast the values of élite groups. In these ways the state and its corporate allies are able to inhibit working class dissent. Rather than a medium through which working class aspirations can be realized, or a neutral arena in which the various interest groups in a pluralist society reach compromise, the state and its apparatuses are portrayed as agencies of social control – control of the working class, a theme developed at length by Ralph Miliband in his examination of *The State in Capitalist Society*.[45]

Alan Fox is an interesting convert to the incorporation viewpoint since he was formerly a prominent member of the 'Oxford School' and associated with its liberal/pluralist analyses of industrial relations. Subsequently Fox has recanted and criticized the pluralist position, objecting that it unrealistically assumes a balance of power. In practice, Fox now argues, power is unbalanced in the employers' favour, and negotiations can only marginally improve the workers' situation.[46] Pluralism, Fox contends, is an ideology that serves to confine workers' aspirations and blinds them to the reality of their predicament.

Exponents of this incorporation theory insist that the working class cannot be quelled into total acquiescence. Workers' everyday experiences tell them that they are a working class, unjustly denied the privileges available to others. From the results of interviews with ninety-one male heads of households in Liverpool, Webb[47] argues that the hegemony of conservative ideas is not total, but that working class dissent only dents a conservative consensus, whilst from a secondary analysis of surveys conducted in Britain and the United States, Michael Mann similarly concludes that dominant values are sufficiently pervasive to prevent a coherent radical ideology binding the working class into a revolutionary force.[48]

Incorporation theorists agree that the position of the working class is inherently unstable. In his work on industrial relations, Hyman[49] recognizes the constant pressures towards incorporation that are exerted through trade unions but he dismisses the possibility of the working class becoming completely pacified. He argues that conflict between capital and labour is too divisive, and that the workers' day-to-day experiences in industry are too alienating. In addition to being an apparatus of incorporation, therefore, Hyman insists that trade unionism is simultaneously a movement of resistance.

Several recent studies of the Labour Party have drawn attention to the ambiguities inherent in its position. Panitch[50] argues that ever since its inception the Labour Party has been committed to an integrative role, meaning that whilst claiming to represent the working class it has also aspired to be a national party, aiming to incorporate the working class into the wider society rather than to spearhead a class war. Since the Second World War, escalating wage demands have posed problems for capitalism, and Labour has responded with the integrative strategy *par excellence*. Rather than politicizing industrial conflict, the Party has offered the trade unions a role in policy-making – in exchange for wage restraint. Panitch argues that the more integrative its own policies become, the more social conflict is displaced to within the Labour Party. Hence the persistent problem of party unity. In Panitch's view, unity could only be achieved if the Party abandoned its integrative role and became an uncompromisingly class organization. Minkin[51] has also drawn attention to the fragility of the Labour Party's 'compacts', pointing to the ever-present potential conflict between Parliamentary leaders who are endeavouring to cultivate a national appeal, and specifically working class interests.

A dispute within the incorporation school concerns the likelihood of the working class 'breaking out'; developing the revolutionary consciousness that would transform the power structure and the socio-economic framework. No one argues that this is absolutely impossible or that it is likely to happen tomorrow, but assessments range from optimism to pessimism. Michael Mann is amongst the pessimists. His study of *Consciousness and Action in the Western Working Class*[52] directly addresses the question as to whether the working class is still a potentially revolutionary force, and Mann's answer is a mildly qualified 'No'. According to Mann, workers' beliefs and attitudes are dualistic. Perceptions of conflict in industry are off-set by the imprint of dominant values. In Mann's view, the development of genuine class consciousness would require energetic propaganda from a socialist vanguard, initially composed largely of intellectuals, and in Britain such a powerful vanguard is conspicuously absent, the 'left' having been isolated from mainstream working class politics by a reformist Labour Party and an economistic trade union movement. Tony Lane argues along broadly similar lines in his study of the role of trade unions.[53] He argues that whilst the grass-roots impulse upon which trade unionism is based arises from a recognition of conflict in the employment relationship, by their nature trade unions can only accommodate labour to capital. He rejects the idea of leaders betraying the rank-and-file. The disappointment of working class aspirations, in Lane's view, is inevitable given the nature of trade unionism, which involves accepting the existence of employers with whom to bargain. This diagnosis parallels Miliband's argument; that the moment the Labour Party accepted 'bourgeois' parliamentary procedures it lost its capacity to be a revolutionary instrument.[54] Both Miliband and Lane insist that the fulfilment of authentic working class aspirations will require a political movement firmly based upon a revolutionary theory – a requirement that the Labour Party seems unlikely to satisfy.

Other writers have taken a more optimistic view. Whereas the current inconsistencies in manual workers' attitudes lead Mann to conclude that working class opposition is unlikely to blossom into

151

full-blooded class consciousness, others have interpreted the same inconsistencies as indicating a potential for change, possibly towards a class-conscious proletariat.[55] Even if the fully class-conscious worker remains the exception, some Marxist writers delight in discovering glimmerings of class awareness that can be construed as steps in the right direction. Between 1963 and 1972 the annual number of days lost due to strikes in Britain rose from under 2 million to over 23 million, whilst the same period saw a leftward shift in the Labour Party and trade union leaderships. Commentators including Westergaard and Resler[56] were able to marshall this as evidence of a possible movement towards revolutionary confrontation. Marxists have always regarded the growth of class consciousness as a complex process which can be interrupted by set-backs. Prior to the development of full class consciousness, Lenin identified a stage of trade union consciousness in which workers in particular trades and firms learnt to recognize common interests and developed a capacity for collective action. Meszaros[57] talks about 'contingent' class consciousness, when only a limited part of the confrontation between labour and capital is perceived, when workers can see little beyond their short-term interests and solidarity develops only amongst localized sections of the labour force. In Meszaros' view, these contingent developments must precede an eventual perception of the unavoidable structural antagonisms that impose 'necessary' directions upon historical change. Beynon coins the concept of 'factory consciousness' in his study of workers at Ford's Halewood plant.[58] Although his loyalties are narrowly focused, the factory-conscious worker is aware of interests shared with other employees in his factory, he is aware that his interests regularly conflict with management's, and is capable of solidaristic action in concert with his fellows. This concept of factory consciousness, together with its counterparts, emphasises the incompleteness of working class incorporation, the unstable character of working class acquiescence, and insists that the foundations exist from which the escalation of a broader class consciousness remains a definite possibility.

Some writers take an optimistic view of the trade unions' revolutionary potential. Whilst Mann talks about trade unions limiting working class aspirations within 'economistic' bounds and containing bargaining within the system without mounting any fundamental challenge to property rights and existing power structures, Hyman argues that even straightforward wage claims are liable to flare into 'control issues', challenging the entire system of ownership and managerial authority if and when it becomes evident that aspirations for improved living standards cannot be realized within the existing economic order.[59] Allen sees no necessary reason why trade unions should not be militant. He criticises the present-day unions for their fragmented structure, their willingness to acknowledge 'national' interests, their slow-moving bureaucracies and their leaders who treat bargaining and compromise as ends in themselves. Allen argues that, to date, the trade unions have been insufficiently militant, but regards conflict as structurally inevitable and, in the longer term, believes that the unions can be instruments for class action and revolutionary change.[60]

Moorhouse and Chamberlain are particularly strident in arguing the possibility of the working class maturing into an effective oppositional force.[61] They interviewed 339 council tenants in Barking, a quarter of whom were participating in a rent strike, and discovered considerable dissent from conservative values. There was widespread disapproval of individuals owning several houses, and sympathy for squatters and factory sit-ins. 75 per cent of those interviewed complained that ordinary people did not have enough say in how the country was run. Moorhouse and Chamberlain wield this evidence to challenge the view that the working class needs converting to socialism by a party with an outside base, such as amongst intellectuals. They argue that ordinary working men and women can develop effective oppositional values amongst themselves, and therefore insist upon the continuing revolutionary potential of the proletariat.

Needless to say, arguments about the possibility of working class opposition blossoming into class consciousness cut little ice with theorists who stress the importance of immediate milieux as determinants of workers' images of society. Their analyses do not suggest that a revolutionary class consciousness awaits the opportunity to break out, contained only by incorporating processes. Pluralists argue that the changed position of the working class has removed both the likelihood and the necessity of a revolutionary response. According to these interpretations, debates about a possible escalation of class consciousness are clutching at misleading straws in the wind.

Pragmatic accommodation

We can distinguish a fourth interpretation of the position of the working class in the power structure. This pragmatic accommodation viewpoint could be treated as a variant within the incorporation theory, but deserves separate consideration. It is not a well-defined school of thought; the following account has been composed by linking evidence and interpretations from several recent studies. But despite this fabrication, there is an important argument here which deserves systematic expression.

Firstly, rather than an all-embracing hegemony of conservative values, this argument goes beyond acknowledging to stress the inconsistencies and contradictions that flaw manual workers' outlooks. Secondly, it regards workers not as normatively committed and convinced that private property together with its surrounding inequalities are morally justified, but as accepting these features of their circumstances pragmatically, as taken-for-granted facts of life. Thirdly, as opposed to arguing that their aspirations and energies are directed into reformist rather than revolutionary channels, this viewpoint stresses the extent to which manual workers accept their circumstances passively and fail to mobilise their potential power in pursuit of any objectives.

The inchoateness that riddles working class culture is a major theme in Nichols and Armstrong's *Workers Divided,* a study of ChemCo, a 'non-militant' plant in southern England.[62] Nichols and Armstrong argue that the weakness of trade unionism at ChemCo and the workforce's lack of cohesion did not indicate an uncomplicated acquiescence. Particular individuals and groups had a variety of strongly-felt grievances. The problem at ChemCo was that the workers were divided; by grade, sex, race and competition for overtime. In addition, bargaining procedures took key issues including wages to a national negotiating level thereby removing local bases for solidarity.* These 'contradictions' in the workers' situations were reflected in their attitudes. Men who complained about the lethargy of their own union criticised more militant workers in other industries for being too greedy, whilst women employees rather than management were blamed by men who felt they had to carry an undue share of the heavy work. Nichols and Armstrong argue that these inconsistencies made it impossible for the workers to understand the structural sources of their troubles and the possibilities for change.

Michael Mann also stresses the ideological confusion that abounds in working class culture. Following an investigation conducted jointly with R. M. Blackburn amongst 941 non-skilled manual workers in Peterborough which probed respondents' views on a battery of industrial and political issues, it was concluded that, 'Neither the workers as a whole nor any identifiable sub-group possessed a coherent belief system.'[63] In the investigators' judgement, the typical worker did not possess *any* coherent understanding of his society, nor did he experience any need for such an understanding. According to Mann and Blackburn, all a worker needs to recognize is a factual need to comply with the particular demands to which he is subject.

One body of opinion regards the maintenance of order in any society as something of a miracle. How can human beings who are capable of independent thought and action be persuaded to conform with any society's requirements? To some observers this question seems especially pertinent in capitalist societies where, if they thought about it, the mass of the people might realize that they are subject to unjust and unnecessary deprivations. How can people be induced to accept social arrangements in which they are denied the full value of their labour, denied control over the organization of their work and see their labour treated as a commodity? To many writers it appears self-evident

---

*It is worth noting that other writers have envisaged the breakdown of local solidarities as facilitating the spread of broader class loyalties. Nichols and Armstrong imply that local solidarity can help workers to recognize more clearly the class character of the exploitation to which they are subject. Both cases can be argued persuasively. This is one of the many factual disagreements where the true nature of the facts is inherently difficult to establish.

that people will not acquiesce unless definite processes, coercive or ideological, persuade them to do so. Investigators seek out these processes and the incorporation theory claims to find them in politics, industrial relations, education, religion, the mass media and a variety of other settings. This reasoning is based upon an implicit conception of man who is seen as resistant to alienation in the Marxist sense. It is seen as contravening man's nature to be treated as a commodity and for him to be denied control over the product of his work – his creations.

Human beings are complex creatures and it is difficult to deny this Marxist view a grain of truth, but there is another side to human nature. There is a sense in which humans are basically conservative animals. Recent social psychology tells us that man's self-consciousness arises only as a reflection from his social environment, implying a 'natural' harmony between all social orders and the characters of their populations. Studies of slavery[64] and inmates in total institutions[65] illustrate how freely men will internalize the norms of their milieux – they cannot become or remain self-consciously human without these processes occurring. In so far as this view of human nature is valid, an implication is that people, being what they are, will ordinarily adjust to their social contexts unless some alien experience destroys the 'natural' harmony. The fact that so many people adjust to their societies requires no special explanation, but rather that they sometimes fail to do so. No one would deny the prevalance of dissent and opposition in societies such as our own. In changing complex societies, which contain numerous sub-cultures and in which social mobility is not unusual, many individuals will be subject to cross-pressures that result in a lack of congruence between their 'selves' and their immediate environments. But maybe it is to explain this rather than conformity that we need to search furthest beyond the elementary facts of human nature.

Frank Parkin has argued that in modern Britain, even amongst manual workers, Labour Party voting should be considered 'out of line' and 'deviant'.[66] There is considerable substance to this view in so far as there is a normal tendency for individuals to accept the status quo and the party that represents its values. Parkin discusses the dominant value system enshrined in society's major institutions which individuals encounter in everyday life. Deviance, in Parkin's view, only occurs when individuals are protected from this dominant culture by a normative sub-system that acts as a buttress. Working class neighbourhood communities and workplace sub-cultures can offer protective environments but Parkin has subsequently argued that even in these contexts the usual tendency is for dominant values to be negotiated to fit the realities of working class life with the result, for example, that inequalities are accepted fatalistically rather than enthusiastically.[67] Parkin argues that radical meaning systems need to be strenuously propagated by outside agencies – political parties – before an effective working class challenge to dominant institutions will be mounted.

Pragmatic accommodation means that people who live under capitalism will ordinarily accept it as a fact of life, like the geographical terrain, until they are shown that an economy can be organised otherwise. Likewise workers will ordinarily accept their positions as workers and believe that they are best suited to such roles until something is done to prove that they are capable of being different persons. The problems encountered in raising the educational aspirations of working class pupils and their parents illustrate how difficult it can be to release individuals' self-concepts from their everyday circumstances. Ideological dominance need not require values to float from the pens and mouths of a ruling class. Existing structures have a built-in ideological force in so far as individuals can develop ideas about themselves and their society only in relation to these structures. If the propagation of subversive ideologies is inhibited, then the mass of the people will accept their social order as a fact of life, though with no greater moral commitment than they feel towards electricity. This interpretation sees the working class kept in its place not so much by the skilful and manipulative incorporating tactics of dominant strata, as by the inhibition or lack of alternative belief systems that would enable the working class to see beyond its current predicament and recognize the possibilities for change.

Surveys show that political interest and activity is concentrated amongst the middle classes. The data collected in the National Opinion Poll in Table 6.1 reveal approximately two-thirds of a national sample of manual workers claiming to be not very or not at all interested in politics. This passive acceptance of circumstances was evident in the results of Stacey's second study of Banbury in 1966 which involved interviews with over 1,440 respondents.[68] This former marketing centre had become an industrial town, and in the process the traditional culture had broken down to be replaced by a more complex social system. Political influence in the new Banbury was exerted through a network of pressure groups but the majority of the population, and the working class in particular, was detached from these processes. Most people remained non-participant even when decisions had obvious implications for their lives such as proposals to demolish nearby property.

Table 6.1 Occupations and Political Interest

	AB	C1	C2	DE
Percentages saying that they were not very, or not at all, interested in politics	39	50	60	67

Source. National Opinion Polls, 1969.

Studies of political socialization amongst schoolchildren support this interpretation of working class political culture. Dowse and Hughes[69] questioned 621 eleven- to seventeen-year-olds in five secondary schools of different types. Irrespective of the type of school attended, pupils from working class homes were distinguished by their low levels of political knowledge, their disinclination to participate in politics and their tendency to passively reflect their parents' party loyalties. With social class background held constant, attendance at a secondary modern as opposed to a grammar school also proved related to this type of political culture. Overall the Dowse and Hughes research portrayed education as reinforcing an existing working class political culture which was ill-informed and acquiescent. Stradling and Zurick's[70] investigation which covered both primary and secondary school pupils produced comparable findings. In this enquiry the pupils were invited to select 'exemplars' – figures they admired and modelled themselves upon. The predominance of choices from sport and pop culture rather than politics was not surprising, but working class pupils, especially when attending secondary modern schools, were significantly less likely to name party politicians than their middle class peers. Once again, this evidence suggests that working class political culture is distinguished by its passivity. In so far as it is thought about at all, politics is treated as an arena that supplies leaders and decisions, rather than a sphere in which individuals are inclined to actively work for change.

Is sociology asking the right questions?

Would anyone deny some truth to the pragmatic accommodation theory? At the same time, is it not equally clear that the theory cannot claim universal validity? There are manual workers who do not quietly accommodate to the system. Militant shop stewards are not mythical creatures, nor are working class members of the Communist Party. It seems likely that all the theories reviewed have valid points to contribute. Most of their authors acknowledge that the theories are about trends, tendencies and their significance rather than monopolistic claims to truth. There is firm evidence that individuals' immediate circumstances make some difference to their reactions to their class positions. Cotgrove and Vamplew[71] investigated 171 process workers, all doing similar jobs in similar plants but in five different parts of the country. On the various sites the proportions expressing support for the Labour Party ranged from 18 to 77 per cent, and the proportions describing themselves as working class from 41 to 71 per cent. These variations were explicable in terms of the communities in which the workers lived. Those living in predominantly working class areas with long traditions of working class politics were the more likely to align themselves with the working class and support the Labour Party. Immersion in blue-collar social relationships and the culture that arises in these settings strengthens the likelihood of individuals behaving and thinking in ways typical of their class. Yet manual workers' orientations are not *only* responses to their immediate milieux. The pluralist and incorporation theories highlight different aspects of the dual significance of trade unions and the Labour Party. Asking which one theory is right assumes that the position of the working class in the power structure is more straightforward than may really be the case.

If this verdict seems inconclusive, we should recognize that it may be our questions rather than the answers that are mistaken. As stated earlier, the background problem to sociological debate about working class politics has concerned the failure of the Marxist armaggedon to materialise. Maybe sociologists have too readily assumed that if workers were objective observers of their predicaments, as their sociological investigators tend to imagine themselves, they would become class conscious and provoke a transformation of society. Having convinced themselves that a fully aware and rational working class would be a revolutionary force, sociologists concentrate upon identifying the impediments. Some sociologists could usefully recognize that their own view of the working class as an exploited, subordinate stratum might be ideologically slanted rather than pristine science.

Is working class acquiescence necessarily inauthentic? With their concern to examine whole social systems, sociologists should not need reminding that workers are also people, often with families, children, interests in education and as consumers. In these areas of life, manual workers' experiences and aspirations are not clearly distinguished from those of other strata. Even at work, whilst they might share some interests with all members of their class, manual workers also possess interests specific to their own jobs, occupations and firms. The Marxist view of the worker's predicament highlights aspects of his situation, but other aspects can be stressed to offer different yet equally authentic interpretations. Treating the failure of a class-conscious proletariat to emerge as *the* problem requiring sociological attention assumes too arbitrarily that the Marxist view possesses a special affinity with reality.

Sociologists who are also socialists, as many are, obviously find this political philosophy convincing and may be puzzled when others prove less receptive. Difficulties in converting the working class are readily attributed to inauthentic obstacles. In fact there are entirely authentic reasons for manual workers regarding socialism with suspicion. The socialist message is far from self-evidently convincing. How much do manual workers materially stand to gain by transferring private property to public ownership and redistributing property incomes? The immediate gains could not be impressive; workers' real incomes would rise only modestly if at all. Do collective ownership and control increase efficiency and raise living standards? Does socialism offer a better deal at work to manual employees in particular? These are all matter for debate. Does anyone consider the evidence from either nationalized industries in Britain or the socialist world completely persuasive? Sociology is mistakenly transfixed when its endeavours to locate the working class in the power structure remain within a Marxist definition of the problem.

The working class in society and sociology

Overloading the concept

Sociology cannot be accused of neglecting the working class. This is no obscure topic whose tiny corps of investigators must appeal for attention. Rather than withering for want of intellectual nourishment, the working class is in greater danger of suffocation from sociology's embrace. It has proved so appetising a subject that sociology threatens to overload the concept – to make the working class explain too much. Previous chapters should have left little doubt that talk of a working class taps a real cleavage in the social structure. At the same time, it should be equally clear that the working class concept can be so inflated as to over-simplify reality and suggest misleading conclusions.

Let us consider five propositions, all non-controversial; in their own terms none could be seriously disputed. Proposition number one is that the British working class votes Labour. Number two notes that in industry the working class is organized in a trade union movement. Needless to say, these statements are generalizations referring to tendencies in working class behaviour to which there are many exceptions. Given these qualifications, whilst they could be expanded and qualified, the propositions leave little scope for outright opposition. The third proposition is that within working class families, in controlling children, there is an exceptional reliance upon physical as opposed to socio-emotional and symbolic sanctions such as expressions of love and approval. The truth of this statement has been underlined in many of the investigations that were reviewed in Chapter 4[1]. Proposition number four observes that in education working class children are relatively unsuccessful, under-represented in secondary schools' top streams and higher education. Fifthly, working class incomes are obtained principally through labour rather than from the possession of capital.

Taken individually it is difficult to envisage any serious commentator challenging these statements. Scrutinising all the evidence would enlarge and amend each proposition, but would not negate its essential truth. Yet despite their individual validity, meshing the propositions creates an illusion. It conjures an impression of a working class, a distinct section of the population, distinguished from more privileged strata by its lack of property, educational disadvantages, a distinctive style of family life and organized as an oppositional force in trade unions and the Labour Party. There are texts which create the impression that such a working class exists, whereas it does not. The illusion results from verbal sleight of hand. All five propositions are true only if we allow the term working class to mean different things in the different statements.

The working class within which support for trade unions and the Labour Party is concentrated consists of manual workers and their families. The section of the population where the use of physical sanctions upon children is exceptionally prevalent is a lower, non-skilled working class. Educational success gradually increases as the occupational scale is ascended with no clear break at any level. The distribution of private property follows yet a different pattern. Here the working class that is so propertyless that it must rely upon labour for its livelihood encompasses over 90 per cent of the population. Coalescing these conceptions of the working class distorts the true facts of life. It might help literary and theoretical coherence but it also lessens sociology's links with reality when the working class concept is stretched to conceal these complexities.

With its use realistically limited, the working class becomes a powerful concept. Its power stems from drawing attention to a syndrome of inequalities that roughly but decisively separate the manual and white-collar labour forces. On one side of this line, work means fundamentally the sale of labour power, the wage packet is embellished with few fringe benefits, there are few opportunities for career progression and workers are persistently on the receiving end of authority. As a reflection of these material inequalities, people's reactions to the system of stratification tend to split the population depending on their sides of the white-blue-collar schism. On the manual side individuals mostly describe themselves as working class, support the Labour Party and are organized in trade unions. The existence of ambiguous cases that are difficult to place is no indictment of the working class concept. There are individuals in what have traditionally been considered white-collar jobs whose circumstances and orientations are proletarian, just as there are blue-collar workers whose life-styles and attitudes are bourgeois. As previous chapters have stressed, the boundaries at the fringe of the working class are blurred. Notwithstanding this, the rule holds that a syndrome of inequalities and individuals' responses hang together in a way that continues to separate a working class from superordinate strata. Defined so as to spotlight this schism, the working class is a theoretical concept which illuminates a real social phenomenon, but in proclaiming the concept's virtues it is important to recognize that there are dimensions of inequality that the division does not tap. This cleavage does not divide the propertied from the remainder of the population, neither is it co-terminous with exclusion from educational privilege, nor does it correspond with all major variations in patterns of family life and uses of leisure. Over-working the concept to encompass the entire spectrum of inequalities only dilutes its value.

False stereotypes

Even with its boundaries realistically set, there are dangers of the working class being misunderstood. Some dangers arise from treating the exceptional as typical. For example, in general, manual jobs offer fewer satisfactions than white-collar occupations, but it is false to regard the monotonous assembly-line as typical blue-collar employment. Assembly-line work, as in motor vehicle plants, is boring and monotonous, and has been repeatedly studied because it is an extreme case. It starkly illustrates how tedious and repetitive factory work can be. What can be forgotten when reading studies of this extreme case, is that less than 2 per cent of the labour force is engaged on mechanized line or belt work. Amongst manual workers the assembly line is infamous. They insist that no money would tempt them to become car-workers and the vast majority are able to avoid the fate. Cases where work is a central life interest are also exceptions, but the majority of blue-collar employees do not experience work as tedious monotony. Many, particularly in skilled occupations, derive some intrinsic satisfactions, whilst others value the company and sociability of the workplace. It is false to think of the working class as so alienated that the mass of the people are awaiting a revolution to transform work or to rid their lives of it completely. These are not common working class aspirations. Even in our notorious car assembly plants, it is difficult to phrase questions to dissuade the majority of workers from expressing job satisfaction.

Another misleading stereotype arises from exaggerating the extent to which manual occupations are devoid of opportunities for career progression. In this respect the contrast between white- and blue-collar employment is sufficiently clear to require no exaggeration. Once again, generalizations from assembly-lines are misleading. In car plants the structure of the labour force, with its low proportion of supervisory posts, rules out career advancement for all but a few. Elsewhere opportunities are not so limited. Apprentices progress to become tradesmen, whilst other workers rise to chargehand, foreman or supervisor. Some even rise into the ranks of management and self-employment. A more common experience is to move into a job offering decent pay and conditions in a good firm that is able to offer reasonable security. These experiences of career progression are modest by middle class standards, and it is right to emphasise the contrast. But it is only from a middle class perspective that one can portray manual workers spending their life-times doing essentially the same jobs. Few talk about their own working lives in these terms. Manual workers attach some importance to 'getting on', value their past achievements and are reluctant to forfeit their career gains.[2]

A further misleading stereotype follows interpreting density of trade union membership amongst manual workers as indicating their commitment to a class struggle. Strikes, sabotage and other forms of unrest attract newspaper headlines and researchers. To place these studies in perspective, it is important to bear in mind that the majority of trade unionists have never been on strike in their lives. Even during 1971–3 when British industry was unusually strike-prone, 97:8 per cent of all establishments remained strike-free, and 80 per cent of manual employees worked in these plants. There are notoriously strike-prone industries including vehicle assembly and the docks, but for most manual workers strikes are events that involve other people, inconvenience other workers and consumers, and which are read about in the press.

Many members are trade unionists in little more than a nominal sense. Surveys reveal the operation of a closed shop as the most common explanation of membership.[3] This does not mean that these members are coerced and reluctant unionists. It means simply that many members join without any ideological commitment. Union membership is often regarded as a condition of employment, like occupational pension schemes. Trade union activists are exceptional creatures. For shop stewards and branch officials, trade unionism can mean something special. They become versed in their organizations' procedures and customs. For the stalwarts, the union can become a way of life and a belief system that makes heavy demands upon time and energy. On average shop stewards commit six hours per week of their own time to union work.[4] Few complain. If they felt that the effort was not worthwhile they would abandon their offices. Being a shop-floor representative can be intrinsically satisfying and offers a sense of serving one's fellows. For some there is the additional feeling of working towards a better society. Although there are senses in which activists reflect more general grass-roots aspirations it is disingenuous to overlook the fact that the activists are a small minority. The majority of trade unionists never contemplate standing for office. When the possibility is suggested their comments indicate distaste for a 'thankless' and 'unrewarding' job whose holder is always liable to be left 'carrying the can', the target for any grievances that arise and prove difficult to resolve.[5] Studies that glean insights into the views of broader labour forces from activists must be mistrusted. Trade union activists are always liable to be untypical, as their memberships know from personal experience. Even amongst union members, surveys uncover widespread suspicions and complaints of excessive trade union power.[6]

This evidence cannot be dismissed as the effects of bourgeois propaganda. Trade unionists know from personal experience how little control they exert over their leaders' statements and actions.

Similar comments can be made regarding working class allegiance to the Labour Party. Labour is certainly the most popular choice amongst the working class, but the depth of its popularity is questionable. At every general election since 1950 the numbers of manual workers not voting at all or for another party have exceeded Labour voters. The bulk of the working class is not sufficiently loyal to Labour even to support the party at the ballot box, whilst the activists who join and work for the party are a tiny fraction of their class.

The above remarks are not intended to dispute that the working class is denied the levels of satisfaction from work and career opportunities that are available in middle class occupations. Neither is it being denied that working class opposition to the prevailing order is persistently liable to disrupt industrial harmony, nor that aspirations for collective betterment are articulated through trade unions and the Labour Party. The argument is simply that focusing upon extreme instances can construct a misleading picture. Extreme cases are useful in illustrating how the middle and working classes differ, but characterizing the manual workforce as simmering with discontent at work, denied all hopes and opportunities for career advancement, immersed in conflict in the work situation, and bound into an industrial and political labour movement is misleading. It may create an appealing and easily comprehensible picture, but one that is untrue in reality.

Ideal types

Further misunderstanding of the working class can arise from sociologists' use of ideal types. Like other academics, sociologists are rational creatures. They prefer their ideas and theories to possess coherence and consistency. Hence sociology's interest in people's 'images of society', typifications of proletarian, deferential and privatized workers, and distinctions between class conscious, factory conscious and trade union conscious employees. These concepts are useful provided we realise that we are trading in theoretical constructs –

unrealistically coherent typifications of actual phenomena. Problems arise when the types are mistaken for reality. As they become involved in academic debates, sociologists easily lull themselves into the belief that sections of the manual labour force really do possess consistently proletarian and deferential orientations.

At best sociology's ideal types identify tendencies. Surveys of manual workers repeatedly unearth muddled and ambiguous attitudes, and this is not because the evidence is contaminated by ineffective research techniques. In real life manual workers (and white-collar workers as well) often subscribe to contradictory viewpoints, and this is an aspect of reality that sociology needs to confront. Their subjects' thinking is rarely as coherent as sociological theorists'.

Fieldworkers invariably have difficulty when they attempt to fit real people into the standard typological boxes.[7] As mentioned earlier, one member of the research team has subsequently explained how much of the evidence collected in *The Affluent Worker* project was inconsistent with the theoretical categories employed to handle the data.[8] Real workers repeatedly puzzle sociologists who attempt to make coherent sense of their attitudes and behaviour. For example, the interviews with Wallsend shipbuilding workers recorded generally favourable attitudes towards jobs and management, but this did not prevent a strike erupting during the research programme.[9] Following the survey amongst non-skilled manual workers in Peterborough that was referred to in the previous chapter, Mann and Blackburn attempted to classify respondents' attitudes along a simple left–right continuum, only to conclude that the exercise was impossible – the workers were too inconsistent.[10] It is easy when reporting research to dwell upon the statistically significant or otherwise meaningful findings, and to ignore the evidence that does not fit. Such practices lend coherence to sociological accounts of the working class, but in the process the arguments lose authenticity. As Nichols and Armstrong rightly insist, sociology needs to stress rather than ignore the contradictions, inchoateness and incompleteness – the divided character of workers' beliefs and attitudes.[11]

It can sound plausible to argue that workers are only temporarily confused by values and meanings that contradict their everyday experience but which emanate from superordinate strata and are constantly diffused through education, the mass media, religious organizations and 'bourgeois' political parties. Given time and the right crisis coupled with appropriate leadership, it has been argued, the working class will perceive the reality of its situation and coalesce into proletarian solidarity. Unfortunately the opposite argument can be couched in equally plausible terms. As incomes continue to rise, home-ownership spreads and middle class life-styles enter the reach of more manual workers, might not the vestiges of working class identities and values be abandoned? It is more likely that for the foreseeable future the working class will continue to interpret and react to its predicaments in ambiguous ways. One general fact of working class life is that individuals are rarely under pressures requiring them to iron out the inconsistencies and blend their ideas into coherent shapes. Individuals may never confront the contradictions in their own attitudes and behaviour. The survey interview may be one of the few occasions when people are prompted to think systematically about work, class and politics. In everyday life individuals are quite capable of harbouring contradictory attitudes. When bargaining to improve their own piece-rates, individuals will be aware of a need to struggle against employers, but when other groups display similar militancy they can be criticised for overturning fair differentials. During the 1970 Pilkington strike, when interviewed, the chairman of the unofficial strike committee declared himself in favour of legislation to outlaw unofficial stoppages.[12] People who make a profession out of understanding or endeavouring to change the world need to resolve the contradictions in their points of view, but this is not the situation of the ordinary working man. Inchoateness and ambiguity are pervasive features of working class culture, and when sociological ideal types obscure this fact they do a disservice to their subject.

Whose side are we on?

Sociology has lost much of the vision that surrounded the subject's birth. The sociological theories of Comte, Marx, Spencer and Durkheim were inspired by historical vision. These theories were developed, not

169

purely for academic interest but to uncover the laws of history thereby enabling mankind to see more clearly how progress towards a better life could be sustained. On a different level, the tradition of empirical research that also matured during the nineteenth century had a similar aim. The fact-gathering of the Factory Inspectors, Public Health Commissions and the early poverty surveys was grounded in the belief that once the facts became known, action and improvement would follow. In the process of becoming an academic subject sociology has lost much of its social purpose. Today there are more people doing sociology for sociology's sake; fewer for society's sake. It is not only sociology that has changed. There has been a parallel change of mood in society-at-large. The Victorian era was a time of optimism. Inspired by the productive power of industrialism, citizens could envisage a time when men would live in prosperity, freedom and harmony. The twentieth century has shattered earlier illusions. Two world wars have destroyed faith in the inevitability of progress. The affluent society may satisfy man's basic needs, but we know that it also generates a new spectrum of wants that can accentuate feelings of deprivation. Between the wars western optimists could cast excited hopes towards the Russian Bolsheviks. Subsequently we learnt the truth about Stalin. Following its landslide victory in 1945 the Labour Party set about recasting the class structure. Coalminers celebrated the nationalization of their industry, equality of educational opportunity was proclaimed and the welfare state declared social security from cradle to grave. By the 1960s social scientists were charting how little had altered. Who knows where we are now heading? Politics has lost its poetry. Do we even know what we would wish our society to be like as the twenty-first century dawns? Trade union leaders appear to see little beyond the next pay round whilst politicians' visions stop at the next general election. As for sociology, it is now written for the profession and its captive audience of students.

This can be frustrating. Many students want to be committed. They expect more from sociology than a route through degree factories. And their professors would love to supply interest and excitement. Hence the self-flagellation. Grand theory and naive empiricism are simultaneously indicted. Students dash through the latest 'ologies and 'isms, and in the absence of living *gurus* the search turns to sociology's roots. Durkheim, Weber and Marx, particularly the young Marx, are constantly reappraised. Amidst this *ennui*, the working class serves as a repository of inspiration. Examining the working class enables sociologists to take sides. Vicarious gratification abounds. The inner-cities and factories must surely harbour problems worth fighting. Working class unrest – the strikes, sit-ins and rent-withholding – appear to offer at least a glimpse of forces that could unlock a better future.

Enthusiasm for the working class easily runs amok. Managers are interested in research on industrial disputes. They want to learn the causes of unrest in order to take preventive action. To many sociology students, in contrast, the causes of unrest are self-evident. The surprising thing is that strikes are so infrequent. From studies of disputes they want to learn how working class militancy is set ablaze, and how it might be kindled elsewhere. How mistaken can you be? Strikes can be stimulating for their 'generals' and assorted observers – the pressmen, television personnel and sociologists. For workers there is nothing heroic about industrial disputes. They are financially damaging and psychologically depressing. Being on strike is boring. After a few days the holiday atmosphere evaporates. Industrial unrest is unpopular amongst the working class.[13]

The old utopias have proved hollow. Does anyone still believe that the replacement of private property by public ownership transforms the position of the working class? Advocating more generous welfare provision is an equally precarious strategy in the class struggle. Recent experience tells us that the cost has to be borne through taxation by the working class. Yet the cause of the working class seems to supply a never-ending stream of issues on which to crusade.

Improving the quality of working life is a currently fashionable cause. Seeking to eradicate meaningless work is an uncontroversially laudable project. Everyone will vote for the principle of job satisfaction and against alienation. Unfortunately the real world forces hard choices. It is pointless to condemn materialism when the wealth enabling sociologists to contemplate and students to study comes from manufacturing industry, and manual workers are as appreciative as any other section of the community of the material well-being that modern industry allows. There is a sense in which the labour market acts as a quasi-experimental situation. If workers themselves placed an over-riding value on job satisfaction, it would pay capitalist employers to offer satisfying jobs since they would attract labour at a sufficiently low cost to compensate for sacrificing more orthodox styles of technological and organizational efficiency. We know how workers vote with their feet, and they are not being deluded to negate their real interests. Workers are also consumers and it is not unreasonable that they should attach greater priority to their standards of life outside the work-place than the quality of working life. Even the most hard-headed managers will agree that, other things remaining equal, job satisfaction should be maximized. The problem is that in industry all other things obstinately refuse to remain equal. Workers know this from everyday experience. Trade unions have not been in the forefront of the movement to improve the quality of working life, and this is a reflection rather than a denial of working class aspirations.

Workers control is another fashionable slogan. It can appear to contain solutions to all the problems of work. Yet if we judge by the interest they display in controlling their own organizations, the trade unions, the stark conclusion must be that few workers are interested in exercising control. Studies of experiments in workers' control point to the same conclusion. In the John Lewis Partnership[14] and the Scott-Bader Commonwealth,[15] the majority of workers stubbornly insist upon behaving like conventional employees.

It is possible to attribute all this to an oppressive capitalist culture. In their families, education and experience of industry, workers learn to expect treatment as employees in jobs that will not be fulfilling. Notwithstanding this, sociologists are not really siding with the working class when their search for commitment obscures workers' real aspirations and problems. There is a difference between taking sides with the working class, and capturing the working class to fill sociology's own ideological void. Like industrial workers, sociologists do not know how industry, based upon modern technology with all its attendant administrative problems, can be organized so as to diffuse power amongst large labour forces, or to offer personally enriching experiences to all employees. Declaring oneself in favour of these objectives may be satisfying, but it is precious little use to the working class.

Working class interests and aspirations

We know less about the aspirations of manual workers than we sometimes care to think. As a result of research, mostly conducted only during the last fifteen years, we are more knowledgeable than previously. Yet there remains a credibility gap between the working class as featured in many sociological texts and the working class that labours in the nation's factories. It is easy for an academic subject to become so obsessed with its own theories, stereotypes and typologies as to lose sight of ordinary workers, and it is equally easy to confuse an ability to converse in Marxist jargon with a genuine understanding of the working class.

We need to constantly remind ourselves why the working class is a topic of habitual concern. The working class has problems because it is denied a whole range of middle class privileges and therefore acts as an oppositional force in society, thereby posing problems for others. Whilst predictions of working class discontents being blended into a coherent revolutionary ideology offering a vision of an alternative and better society remain utopian, it is equally unrealistic to expect workers to see sense, middle class style, cooperate harmoniously with managements and accept pay norms that reduce their standards of living in the 'national interest'. Blue-collar workers' situations say otherwise. Manual workers have to struggle to maintain their prerogatives and incomes at work, and will continue to demand improvements through the political system.

Economic security remains a major problem for the working class. This is not an issue of the past but a living concern for working class people, and not only when the economy is depressed. In industry, manual workers have to fight a constant battle to keep real earnings edging up rather than down. To beat inflation the shop-floor has to bargain. Blue-collar workers are not protected by the salary scales and progressive careers that the middle classes enjoy. Piecework, bonus and measured daywork systems are considered necessary to motivate factory employees and offer endless scope for bargaining. The threats of redundancy and short-time are never far from the horizon even when the economy is booming. Working class affluence is no myth. In printing, construction and other industries it is not difficult to find blue-collar pay-slips that excite the middle classes to envy. Households containing more than one wage-earner and no dependents can well afford holidays abroad and other luxuries. The problem for blue-collar families is that their middle class standards are never secure. Most blue-collar families now enjoy incomes well above the officially defined poverty level. The poor and the working class are not synonymous expressions. In Britain the problem of relative poverty is concentrated amongst low wage-earners with several dependents, and the economically inactive who are entirely dependent upon state benefits. There is a sense, however, in which regarding poverty as a minority problem is unrealistic. Seeing one's living standards plunge beneath the poverty line is a risk shared by the entire working class. At particular stages in the life-cycle, particularly the child-rearing phase and retirement, it is difficult for manual families to avoid this fate. Misfortunes such as chronic ill health and redundancy, which individuals are helpless to avoid, also leave the working class dependent upon the state's safety net. The middle classes are largely removed from risk by that other welfare state comprising occupational fringe benefits and privately financed social services. Recipients of this largess appear to avoid both the 'scrounger' label and the finance of their services being defined as a drain that the economy can ill afford. That the services upon which the working class is dependent are discussed in these terms indicates how far we remain from making genuine economic security a right of citizenship.

Manual workers' interest in security finds various expressions. Restrictive practices appear inappropriately labelled when the alternative is to work oneself out of a job. Grass-roots support for public ownership, import controls and government subsidies to industry largely expresses a demand for job security. Car workers were never prominent supporters of nationalization until first at Chrysler then British Leyland the disappearance of their jobs became imminent. Britain remains two nations as far as economic security is concerned and still awaits a concerted attack on this problem.

Housing is another area where the working class possesses distinct interests and where the problem is often defined for public discussion in other than working class terms. For the minorities who occupy slums and multi-tenanted premises, and particularly for the homeless, housing is clearly a provocative issue. Amongst the middle class housing is also a problem though the details are entirely different. Here the concern is focused upon the supply and price of mortgages. The bulk of the working class, however, is excluded from the private, owner-occupied housing market; raising a deposit and meeting the repayments during the early years of a mortgage's life are simply out of the question for many working class families. For this reason, manual workers form the bulk of a 'housing class' that possesses distinct interests. Working class housing chances depend greatly upon council house building and rent policies. These policies hold a major key to working class life-chances outside the work-place. For the working class, housing is a public issue rather than a purely private, domestic problem. It might seem reasonable to the middle classes, but the working class suffers when public housing programmes and prices are tailored not to housing need but to the requirements of general economic management.

In the housing field the working class is also particularly vulnerable to the planning profession's mistakes and indiscretions. Their problems are more general than the risk of motorways being constructed close to their homes. Modern evangelistic bureaucrats[16] have destroyed dozens of inner-city neighbourhoods, and replaced them with new estates that continue to look quite unlike developments intended for private purchasers. Working class families lack the control that the middle classes expect over the environments in which they live.

A third area where the working class has distinctive interests concerns opportunities for 'getting on'. Most working class parents are not disinterested in their children's education, which does not mean that they favour sweeping changes in the school system. They mostly favour comprehensive reorganization. Secondary moderns attract little support in any strata.[17] However, school education is of particular concern to those sections of the middle class that expect schooling to lead to higher education and commensurate job prospects. Working class ambitions are relatively modest and more easily satisfied by what the schools already offer. Working class parents repeatedly confront researchers singing the praises of their children's schools. Today the majority of working class children leave school with paper qualifications – a level of attainment that was never within their parents' reach. Pupils progress to levels of which their parents are proud. Entering employment at sixteen with a handful of CSEs might raise sighs of disappointment in middle class homes, but in working class families it constitutes success. Proposals for positive discrimination in favour of culturally deprived children, and community schools with curricula linked to specifically working class values are not responses to authentic working class aspirations. For the working class, 'getting on' becomes a problem at the end of full-time schooling. Since the Robbins Report in 1963 the number of places in higher education has more than doubled, and the Open University has opened a new supply of second chances. In contrast, the proportions of beginning workers able to enter apprenticeships and opportunities for day release have remained stagnant. In the past the 'alternative route' has been an important channel for upward mobility for individuals commencing their careers in working class occupations. Overall developments in education and patterns of recruitment to management and the professions have consolidated opportunity structures used principally by the middle classes and left manual workers, if anything, increasingly disadvantaged.

These comments do not climax with a political manifesto for the working class. The more modest intention is to indicate directions which discussion and research can fruitfully follow. Despite the volume of study that the working class has attracted, redundancy, unemployment, housing, apprenticeships and further education have not featured amongst the most popular research areas. Yet it is in these directions that sociology needs to look if it wants to side with the working class. Concern for the problems of the working class need not rest wholly upon sympathy with the underdog. Enlightened self-interest gives all sections of the public a stake in having working class discontents articulated and serviced. Effective government and revitalising British industry depend upon working class interests being competently represented. Sociology has a role to play in developing a better understanding of the working class, but playing this role requires that sociologists tune in to the appropriate issues. Whilst sociologists are unlikely to neglect the working class, the sheer weight of concern threatens to distort the subject-matter. These are dangers in stretching the working class concept too widely, developing falsely exaggerated stereotypes and propagating unrealistically smooth ideal types. There are further dangers of mistaken identity in sociologists' desire for commitment vicariously enrolling the working class behind causes that bear little resemblance to manual workers' aspirations. Sociology should not expect too much from the working class. If studies of redundancy, housing and further education seem unlikely to restore sociology's sense of historical purpose, the implication is that the subject needs to look beyond the working class for this kind of inspiration.

References and further reading

Chapter 1 The debate about the working class

1. J. Westergaard and H. Resler, *Class in a Capitalist Society*, Heinemann, 1975.

2. Ibid., p. 17.

3. Ibid., p. 53.

4. I. C. Jarvie, *Concepts and Society*, Routledge, 1972.

5. Ibid., p. 101.

6. Ibid., pp. 119–20.

7. Examples include W. G. Runciman, *Relative Deprivation and Social Justice*, Routledge, 1966.

8. P. Hiller, 'Continuities and variations in everyday conceptual components of class', *Sociology*, 9 (1975) 255.

9. H. F. Moorhouse, 'Attitudes to class and class relationships in Britain', *Sociology*, 10 (1976) 469.

10. H. Popitz et al., 'The workers's image of society', in T. Burns (ed.), *Industrial Man*, Penguin, 1969.

11. See H. F. Moorhouse op. cit., and G. Mackenzie, 'World images and the world of work', in G. Esland et al., (eds), *People and Work*, Holmes McDougall, 1975.

12. D. Webb, 'Some reservations on the use of self-rated class', *Sociological Review*, 21 (1973) 321.

13. See K. Roberts et al., *The Fragmentary Class Structure*, Heinemann, 1977.

14. R. Price and G. S. Bain, 'Union growth revisited: 1948–1974 in perspective', *British Journal of Industrial Relations*, 14 (1976) 339.

15. See K. Roberts et al., op. cit.

16. See M. Abrams et al., *Must Labour Lose?*, Penguin, 1960; W. G. Runciman op. cit., and K. Roberts et al., op. cit.

17. C. Rallings, 'Some thoughts on the political consequences of the growing white-collar proletariat'. Paper presented to conference on *The Middle Class in Mass Politics,* University of Salford, 1977.

18. D. Jary et al., *The Middle Class Left in Britain and Australia,* Department of Sociological and Political Studies, University of Salford, 1976.

19. See K. Roberts et al., op. cit.

20. S. M. Lipset and R. Bendix, *Social Mobility in Industrial Society*, Heinemann, 1959.

21. A. Sturmthal, *White-collar Trade Unions,* University of Illinois Press, 1967.

22. D. Rose and D. Urwin, 'What are parties based on?', *New Society,* 7 May 1970.

23. J. H. Goldthorpe, 'Social stratification in industrial society', in M. M. Tumin (ed.), *Readings on Social Stratification*, Prentice-Hall, 1970.

24. P. Hollander, *Soviet and American Society,* Oxford University Press, 1973.

25 A. Giddens, *The Class Structure of the Advanced Societies,* Hutchinson, 1953.

26. F. Parkin, *Class Inequality and Political Order*, MacGibbon and Kee, 1971.

27. S. Wesolowski, 'The notions of strata and class in socialist society', in A. Beteille (ed.), *Social Inequality,* Penguin, 1969.

28. D. Lane, *The End of Inequality,* Penguin, 1971.

29. D. Lane, *The Socialist Industrial State,* Allen and Unwin, 1976.

30. S. Wesolowski, op. cit.

31. B. Barber, *Social Stratification,* Harcourt Brace and World, 1957.

32. D. H. Wrong, 'Social inequality without social stratification', in D. H. Wrong and H. L. Gracey (eds), *Readings in Introductory Sociology,* Macmillan, 1972.

33. This perspective is used in W. G. Runciman, op. cit.

Chapter 2 Work

1. For evidence and illustrations see K. Roberts et al., *The Fragmentary Class Structure,* Heinemann, 1977.

2. A. I. Harris and R. Clausen, *Labour Mobility in Britain, 1953–63,* HMSO, 1966.

3. See M. Wynn, *Family Policy,* Penguin, 1972.

4. See K. Roberts et al., op. cit.

5. S. Parker, 'The effects of redundancy', in G. Esland et al. (eds), *People and Work,* Holmes McDougall, 1975.

6. D. Marsden and E. Duff, *Workless,* Penguin, 1975.

7. Reported in *The Guardian,* 4 May 1977.

8. M. Leighton, 'Journey into the working class', *Sunday Times,* 6 Jan. 1977.

9. F. Herron, *Labour Market in Crisis,* Macmillan, 1975.

10. S. Parker, op. cit.

11. R. Martin and R. H. Fryer, *Redundancy and Paternalist Capitalism,* Allen and Unwin, 1973; see also M. J. Hill et al., *Men Out of Work,* Cambridge University Press, 1973.

12. T. Nichols, 'The sociology of accidents and the social production of industrial injury', in G. Esland et al., op. cit.

13. M. Lane, 'Explaining educational choice', *Sociology,* 6 (1972) 255.

14. F. Field et al., *To Him Who Hath,* Penguin, 1977.

15. D. Wedderburn and C. Craig, 'Relative deprivation in work', in

D. Wedderburn (ed.), *Poverty, Inequality and Class Structure*, Cambridge University Press, 1974.

16. A. Fox, *Beyond Contract,* Faber and Faber, 1974.

17. A. Fox, 'The meaning of work', in *Occupational Categories and Cultures,* 1, Open University Press, 1976.

18. Ibid.

19. H. Beynon, *Working for Ford,* Penguin, 1973; C. R. Walker and R. H. Guest, *The Man on the Assembly Line,* Harvard University Press, 1952; E. Chinoy, *Automobile Workers and the American Dream,* Beacon, 1965.

20. R. Dubin, 'Industrial workers' worlds: a study of the central life interests of industrial workers', in A. M. Rose (ed.), *Human Behaviour and Social Processes,* Routledge, 1962.

21. A. Fox, op. cit.

22. See J. M. and R. E. Pahl, *Managers and their Wives,* Allen Lane, 1971.

23. A. I. Harris and R. Clausen, op. cit.

24. R. Martin and R. H. Fryer, op. cit.

25. H. Hyman, 'The value systems of different classes', in R. Bendix and S. M. Lipset (eds), *Class, Status and Power*, Routledge, 1967.

26. For a discussion of this issue see K. Roberts, *Leisure,* Longman, 1970.

27. H. L. Wilenski, 'Work as a social problem', in H. S. Becker (ed.), *Social Problems: a modern approach,* Wiley, 1966; G. Friedmann, *The Anatomy of Work,* Heinemann, 1961.

28. J. Hall and D. C. Jones 'Social grading of occupations', *British Journal of Sociology,* 1 (1950) 31.

29. R. H. Turner, 'Life-situation and sub-culture: a comparison of merited prestige judgements by three occupational classes in Britain', *British Journal of Sociology,* 9 (1958) 299.

30. M. Young and P. Willmott, 'Social grading by manual workers', *British Journal of Sociology,* 7 (1956) 337.

31. E. Hughes, 'Work and the self', in J. H. Rohrer and M. Sherif (eds.), *Social Psychology at the Crossroads,* Harper and Row, 1951.

32. M. Sissions, 'The psychology of social class', in *Money, Wealth and Class,* Open University Press, 1971.

33. R. Sennett and J. Cobb, *The Hidden Injuries of Class*, Random House, 1972.

34. M. L. Kohn and C. Schooler, 'Occupational experience and psychological functioning', *American Sociological Review,* 38 (1973) 97.

35. P. Berger, *The Human Shape of Work,* Macmillan, 1964.

36. See G. S. Bain and R. Price, 'Who is a white-collar employee?', *British Journal of Industrial Relations,* 10 (1972) 325.

37. For specific versions see R. Millar, *The New Classes,* Longman, 1965; M. A. and M. W. Westley, *The Emerging Worker,* McGill – Queens University Press, 1973.

38. R. Blauner, *Alienation and Freedom,* University of Chicago Press, 1964.

39. Such as N. A. B. Wilson, *On the Quality of Working Life,* HMSO, 1973; P. Warr and T. Wall, *Work and Well-being,* Penguin, 1975; L. E. Davis and A. B. Cherns (eds), *The Quality of Working Life,* 2 vols, Free Press, 1975.

40. As noted by A. Goyder, 'A note on the declining relationship between objective and subjective class measures', *British Journal of Sociology,* 26 (1975) 102.

41. T. Nichols, 'The "socialism" of management', *Sociological Review,* 23 (1975) 245.

42. See N. Bosquet, 'The Prison Factory', *New Left Review,* 73 (1972) 23.

43. A. Fox, op. cit.

44. J. Kelly, *Is Scientific Management Possible?* Faber, 1968.

45. M. Mann, *Workers on the Move,* Cambridge University Press, 1973.

46. S. Cotgrove et al., *The Nylon Spinners,* Allen and Unwin, 1971.

47. D. Wedderburn and R. Crompton, *Workers' Attitudes and Technology,* Cambridge University Press, 1972.

48. J. H. Goldthorpe et al., *The Affluent Worker, Vol. 1. Industrial Attitudes and Behaviour,* Cambridge University Press, 1968.

49. D. Braverman, *Labour and Monopoly Capital,* Monthly Review Press, 1974.

50. J. Chadwick-Jones, *Automation and Behaviour,* Wiley, 1969.

51. As alleged by J. Westergaard and H. Resler, *Class in a Capitalist Society,* Heinemann, 1975

52. See D. Jary et al., *The Middle Class Left in Britain and Australia,* Department of Sociological and Political Studies, University of Salford, 1976; C. Rallings, 'Some thoughts on the political consequences of the growing white-collar proletariat.' Paper presented to conference on *The Middle Class in Mass Politics,* University of Salford, 1977; and K. Roberts et al., *The Fragmentary Class Structure,* Heinemann, 1977.

Chapter 3 Socio-economic trends: is the working class in decline?

1. G. Routh, *Occupations and Pay in Great Britain, 1906–1960,* Cambridge University Press, 1965.

2. A. Tropp, *The School-teachers,* Heinemann, 1957.

3. D. Lockwood, *The Black-coated Worker,* Allen and Unwin, 1958.

4. W. G. Runciman, *Relative Deprivation and Social Justice,* Routledge, 1966.

5. K. Roberts et al., *The Fragmentary Class Structure,* Heinemann, 1977.

6. B. C. Roberts et al., *Reluctant Militants*, Heinemann, 1972.

7. T. Lane and K. Roberts, *Strike at Pilkingtons*, Fontana, 1971.

8. Glasgow University Media Group, *Bad News*, Routledge, 1976.

9. A. W. Gouldner, *Wildcat Strike*, Routledge, 1955.

10. W. A. and M. W. Westley, *The Emerging Worker*, McGill – Queens University Press, 1973.

11. D. Lane, *The End of Inequality*, Penguin, 1971.

12. S. Wesolowski, 'The notions of strata and class in socialist society', in A. Beteille (ed.), *Social Inequality*, Penguin, 1969.

13. R. Millar, *The New Classes*, Longman, 1965.

14. F. Zweig, *The Worker in an Affluent Society*, Heinemann, 1961.

15. G. Turner, *The Car Makers*, Eyre and Spottiswoode, 1963.

16. D. Butler and D. Stokes, *Political Change in Britain*, Macmillan, 1969.

17. B. Ineichen, 'Home-ownership and manual workers' life-styles', *Sociological Review*, **20** (1972) 391.

18. W. H. Form, 'The internal stratification of the working class', *American Sociological Review*, **38** (1973) 697.

19. G. Mackenzie, *The Aristocracy of Labour*, Cambridge University Press, 1973.

20. See B. Harrison, *Education, Training and the Urban Ghetto*, John Hopkins University Press, 1972; P. B. Doeringer and M. J. Piore, *Internal Labour Markets and Manpower Analysis*, D. C. Heath & Co., 1971; M. Piore, 'The dual labour market: theory and implications', in D. M. Gordon (ed.), *Theories of Poverty and Underemployment*, Heath-Lexington, 1972.

21. E. H. Phelps-Brown, 'The Influence of trade unions and collective bargaining on pay levels and pay structure', in W. E. G. McCarthy (ed.), *Trade Unions*, Penguin, 1972.

22. J. C. Goyder, 'A note on the declining relationship between

objective and subjective class measures', *British Journal of Sociology,* **26** (1975) 102.

23. D. H. Wrong, 'Social inequality without social stratification', in D. H. Wrong and H. L. Gracey (eds), *Readings in Introductory Sociology,* Macmillan, 1972.

24. J. H. Goldthorpe et al., *The Affluent Worker in the Class Structure,* Cambridge University Press, 1969.

25. Ibid.

26. I. C. Cannon, 'Ideology and occupational community: a study of compositors', *Sociology,* **1** (1967) 165.

27. See K. Roberts et al., op. cit.

28. M. Mann, *Workers on the Move,* Cambridge University Press, 1973.

29. T. S. Chivers, 'The proletarianisation of a service worker', *Sociological Review,* **21** (1973) 633.

30. R. K. Brown and P. Brannen, 'Social relations and social perspectives amongst shipbuilding workers: a preliminary statement', *Sociology,* **4** (1970) 71 and 197; R. K. Brown et al., 'The contours of solidarity; social stratification and industrial relations in shipbuilding', *British Journal of Industrial Relations,* **10** (1972) 12.

31. R. L. Davis and J. M. Cousins, 'The new working class and the old', in M. Bulmer (ed,), *Working Class Images of Society,* Routledge, 1976.

32. R. Moore, *Pitmen, Preachers and Politics,* Cambridge University Press, 1974.

33. R. Blackburn, 'The unequal society', in R. Blackburn and A. Cockburn (eds), *The Incompatibiles,* Penguin, 1967.

34. W. A. and M. W. Westley, op. cit.

35. G. Katona et al., *Aspirations and Affluence,* McGraw–Hill, 1971.

36. A. Levison, *The Working Class Majority,* Coward, McCann and Geoghegan, 1974.

37. P. and B. Sexton, *Blue Collars and Hard Hats,* Random House, 1971.

38. But see N. Bosanquet and P. B. Doeringer, 'Is there a dual labour market in Great Britain?', *The Economic Journal,* **83** (1973) 421.

39. G. Routh, op. cit.

40. B. Abel-Smith and P. Townsend, *The Poor and the Poorest,* Occasional Paper in Social Administration, No. 17, Codicote Press, 1965.

41. B. Jordan, *Paupers,* Routledge, 1973; B. Jordan, *Poor Parents,* Routledge, 1974.

42. K. Joseph, 'The cycle of deprivation', in E. Butterworth and R. Holman (eds), *Social Welfare in Modern Britain,* Fontana, 1975.

43. K. Coates and R. Silburn, *Poverty: the forgotten Englishmen,* Penguin, 1970.

44. R. Boyson, *Down with the Poor,* Churchill Press, 1971.

45. M. Wynn, *Family Policy,* Penguin, 1972.

46. J. C. Kincaid, *Poverty and Equality in Britain,* Penguin, 1973.

47. M. Rutter and N. Madge, *Cycles of Disadvantage,* Heinemann, 1976.

Chapter 4 Family, community and life-styles

1. See N. Dennis et al., *Coal is Our Life,* Tavistock, 1956.

2. M. Young and P. Willmott, *Family and Kinship in East London,* Routledge, 1957. See also J. Platt, *Social Research in Bethnal Green,* Macmillan, 1971. Another influential book was R. Hoggart, *The Uses of Literacy,* Chatto and Windus, 1957.

3. See B. Jackson, *Working Class Community,* Routledge, 1968.

4. See P. Townsend, *The Family Life of Old People,* Routledge, 1961.

5. See M. Young and P. Willmott, op. cit.; C. Vereker et al., *Urban Redevelopment and Social Change,* Liverpool University Press, 1961.

6. J. Gower Davies, *The Evangelistic Bureaucrat*, Tavistock, 1972.

7. P. Willmott, *The Evolution of a Community*, Routledge, 1963.

8. H. Jennings, *Societies in the Making*, Routledge, 1962.

9. N. Dennis, *People and Planning*, Faber and Faber, 1970; N. Dennis, *Public Participation and Planners' Blight*, Faber and Faber, 1972.

10. J. Seabrook, *City Close-Up*, Allen Lane, 1971.

11. C. Rosser and C. Harris, *The Family and Social Change*, Routledge, 1965.

12. M. Young and P. Willmott, *The Symmetrical Family*, Routledge, 1973.

13. J. H. Goldthorpe et al., *The Affluent Worker in the Class Structure*, Cambridge University Press, 1969.

14. See J. Klein, *Samples from English Cultures*, Vol. 2, Routledge, 1965; P. Willmott, *Adolescent Boys of East London*, Routledge, 1966.

15. S. Sharpe, *Just Like a Girl*, Penguin, 1976.

16. G. Murdock, 'Culture and classlessness', paper presented to *Symposium on Work and Leisure*, Salford, 1973.

17. M. Bone, *The Youth Service and Similar Provision for Young People*, HMSO, 1972.

18. R. K. Kelsall et al, *Graduates: the sociology of an elite*, Methuen, 1972.

19. M. Schofield, *The Sexual Behaviour of Young Adults*, Allen Lane, 1973.

20. G. Gorer, *Sex and Marriage in England Today*, Nelson, 1971.

21. For a summary see G. R. Leslie, *The Family in Social Context*, Oxford University Press, 1967.

22. C. Bell, *Middle Class Families*, Routledge, 1968.

23. H. Gavron, *The Captive Wife*, Routledge, 1966.

24. See also N. C. A. Parry and D. Johnson, *Leisure and Social Structure*, Hatfield Polytechnic, 1974.

25. F. Musgrove, *The Migratory Elite*, Heinemann, 1963.

26. D. G. McKinley, *Social Class and Family Life*, Free Press, 1964.

27. J. L. Roach, 'A theory of lower class behaviour', in L. Gross (ed.), *Sociological Theory*, Harper and Row, 1967.

28. M. Kohn, *Class and Conformity*, Dorsey Press, 1969.

29. J. and E. Newson, *Infant Care in an Urban Community*, Allen and Unwin, 1963; J. and E. Newson, *Four Years Old in an Urban Community*, Allen and Unwin, 1968.

30. R. Davie et al., *From Birth to Seven*, Longman, 1972.

31. J. W. B. Douglas et al., 'Delinquency and Social Class', *British Journal of Criminology*, 6 (1966) 294.

32. C. P. Wallis and R. Maliphant, 'Delinquent areas in the County of London: ecological factors', in J. B. Mays (ed), *Juvenile Deliquency, the Family and the Social Group*, Longman, 1972.

33. D. J. West and D. P. Farrington, *Who Becomes Delinquent?*, Heinemann, 1974.

34. S. Box and J. Ford, 'The facts don't fit: on the relationship between social class and criminal behaviour', *Sociological Review*, 19 (1971) 31.

35. W. R. Blytheway and D. R. May, 'On fitting the "facts" of social class and criminal behaviour: a rejoinder to Box and Ford', *Sociological Review*, 19 (1971) 585.

36. L. McDonald, *Social Class and Delinquency*, Faber and Faber, 1969.

37. N. Elias and J. Scotson, *The Established and the Outsiders*, Cass, 1965.

38. C. Gibson, 'The association between divorce and social class in England and Wales', *British Journal of Sociology*, 25 (1974) 79.

39. P. H. Mann, 'Survey of a theatre audience: findings', *British Journal of Sociology,* **18** (1967) 75.

40. P. Hollander, *Soviet and American Society,* Oxford University Press, 1973.

41. E. A. Douvan and J. Adelson, *The Adolescent Experience,* Wiley, 1966.

42. For example, see S. Sharpe, op. cit.

43. G. Gorer, op. cit.

44. B. Ineichen, 'Home-ownership and manual workers' life-styles', *Sociological Review,* **38** (1973), 697.

45. J. H. Goldthorpe et al., op. cit.

Chapter 5 Education

1. B. Jackson, *Streaming: an educational system in miniature,* Routledge, 1966; J. W. B. Douglas, *The Home and the School,* MacGibbon and Kee, 1964.

2. Ibid.

3. J. W. B. Douglas et al., *All our Future,* P. Davies, 1968.

4. Committee on Higher Education, *Higher Education* (Robbins Report), HMSO, 1963.

5. Ibid.

6. J. Ford, *Social Class and the Comprehensive School,* Routledge, 1969.

7. J. Whitburn et al., *People in Polytechnics,* Society for Research into Higher Education, 1976.

8. A. H. Halsey, 'Sociology and the equality debate', *Oxford Review of Education,* 1 (1975) 9.

9. J. W. B. Douglas, *The Home and the School,* op. cit.; J. W. B. Douglas et al., op. cit.

10. R. Davie et al., *From Birth to Seven,* Longman, 1972.

11. D. P. Boyd, 'The educational background of a selected group of England's leaders', *Sociology*, **8** (1974) 305.

12. See A. R. Jensen, *Genetics and Education*, Methuen, 1972; H. J. Eysenck, *The Inequality of Man*, Temple Smith, 1972.

13. This position is advanced in K. Richardson and D. Spears (eds), *Race, Culture and Intelligence*, Penguin, 1972.

14. Both 'hereditarians' and 'environmentalists' have commended the over-view of the subject in P. E. Vernon, *Intelligence and Cultural Environment*, Methuen, 1969.

15. P. G. Squibb, 'The concept of intelligence – a sociological perspective', *Sociological Review*, **21** (1973) 57; C. J. Karier, 'Testing for order and control in the liberal corporate state', *Educational Theory*, **22** (1972) 159.

16. J. W. B. Douglas, op. cit.

17. Central Advisory Council for Education, *15 to 18* (Crowther Report), HMSO, 1959.

18. R. Boudon, *Education, Opportunity and Social Inequality*, Wiley, 1973.

19. J. B. Mays, *Education and the Urban Child*, Liverpool University Press, 1962.

20. B. Jackson and D. Marsden, *Education and the Working Class*, Routledge, 1962.

21. I. K. Birksted, 'School performance viewed from the boys', *Sociological Review*, **24** (1976) 63.

22. R. Greenslade, *Goodbye to the Working Class*, Marion Boyars, 1976.

23. O. Banks and D. Finlayson, *Success and Failure in the Secondary School*, Methuen, 1973.

24. Central Advisory Council for Education, *Children and their Primary Schools* (Plowden Report), HMSO, 1967.

25. J. M. Bynner, *Parents' Attitudes to Education*, HMSO, 1972.

26. M. Young and P. McGeeney, *Learning Begins at Home*, Routledge, 1968.

27. A. H. Halsey, *Educational Priority*, HMSO, 1972.

28. E. Midwinter, *Priority Education*, Penguin, 1972.

29. H. Acland, 'What is a bad school?', *New Society*, 9 Sept. 1971; 'Does parent involvement matter?', *New Society*, 16 Sept. 1971.

30. H. Wilson and G. Herbert, 'Hazards of environment', *New Society*, 8 June 1972.

31. M. Young and P. McGeeney, op. cit.

32. See B. Bernstein, *Class, Codes and Control*, Vol. I, Routledge, 1971.

33. J. Pen, *Income Distribution*, Penguin, 1971, 405–7.

34. J. Klein, *Samples from English Cultures*, Vol 2, Routledge, 1965.

35. D. Henderson, 'Contextual specificity, discretion and cognitive socialisation', *Sociology*, 4 (1970) 311.

36. W. P. Robinson and S. J. Rackstraw, 'Variations in mother's answers to children's questions, as a function of social class, verbal intelligence test scores and sex', *Sociology*, 1 (1967) 259.

37. J. Cook-Gumperz, *Social Control and Socialisation*, Routledge, 1973.

38. B. Bernstein and D. Young, 'Social Class differences in conceptions of the uses of toys', *Sociology*, 1 (1967) 131.

39. J. Jones and B. Bernstein, 'Appendix', in W. Brandis and B. Bernstein, *Selection and Control*, Routledge, 1974.

40. W. Brandis and B. Bernstein, op. cit.

41. D. Lawton, *Social Class, Language and Education*, Routledge, 1968.

42. D. M. and G. A. Gahagan, *Talk Reform*, Routledge, 1970.

43. H. Rosen, *Language and Social Class*, Falling Wall Press, 1972.

44. A. D. Edwards, 'Social class and linguistic choice', *Sociology*, 10 (1976) 101.

45. D. Lawton, op. cit.

46. M. Heber, 'A comparative study of questions asked by two groups

of seven year old boys differing in social class', *Sociology*, 8 (1974) 246.

47. A. J. Wootton, 'Talk in the homes of young children', *Sociology*, 8 (1974) 277.

48. See M. F. D. Young (ed.), *Knowledge and Control*, Collier-Macmillan, 1971.

49. D. Bryne et al., *The Poverty of Education*, Martin Robertson, 1975.

50. Ibid., 2.

51. Ibid., 144.

52. D. J. Pyle, 'Intra-regional variations in educational provision ... some comments on Byrne and Williams', *Sociology*, 9 (1975) 491 53 Central Advisory Council for Education, op. cit.

54. J. W. B. Douglas et al., op. cit.

55. R. Dale et al. (eds), *Schooling and Capitalism*, Routledge, 1976, 1.

56. R. Johnson, 'Notes on the schooling of the English working class', in R. Dale et al., (eds), op. cit.

57. P. G. Squibb, op. cit.; C. J. Karier, op. cit.

58. W. Labov, 'The logic of non-standard English', in N. Keddie (ed.), *Tinker, tailor ... the myth of cultural deprivation*, Penguin, 1973.

59. L. Eisenberg, 'Strengths of the inner-city child', in J. Raynor and J. Harden (eds), *Cities, Communities and the Young*, Routledge, 1973; W. L. Friedman, 'Cultural deprivation: a commentary in the sociology of knowledge', In J. Raynor and J. Harden, op. cit.

60. See N. Keddie (ed.), op. cit.

61. N. Keddie, 'Classroom knowledge', in M. F. D. Young, op. cit.

62. D. Lawton, *Class, Culture and Curriculum*, Routledge, 1975.

63. R. Rosenthal and L. Jacobson, 'Teacher expectancies: determinants of pupils' IQ test gains', *Psychological Reports*, 19 (1966) 115.

64. D. A. Pidgeon, *Expectation and Pupil Performance*, NFER, 1970.

65. J. W. B. Douglas, op. cit.

66. C. Lacey, *Hightown Grammar,* Manchester University Press, 1970.

67. D. Hargreaves, *Social Relations in a Secondary School,* Routledge, 1967.

68. J. W. B. Douglas, op. cit.

69. E. J. Goodacre, *Teachers and their Pupils' Home Backgrounds,* NFER, 1968.

70. N. Keddie, 'Classroom knowledge', op. cit.

71. J. Murphy, 'Teacher expectations and working class under-achievement', *British Journal of Sociology,* 25 (1974) 326.

72. R. Nash, *Classrooms Observed,* Routledge, 1973.

73. M. Lane, 'Explaining educational choice', *Sociology,* 6 (1972) 255.

74. R. H. Turner, *The Social Context of Ambition,* Chandler, 1964; K. Roberts et al., *The Fragmentary Class Structure,* Heinemann, 1977.

75. M. Leighton, 'Journey into the working class', *Sunday Times,* 6 Jan. 1977.

76. R. W. Witkin, 'Social class influence on the amount and type of positive evaluation of school lessons', *Sociology,* 5 (1971) 169.

77. C. Jencks et al., *Inequality,* Allen Lane, 1973

78. R. Boudon, op. cit.

Chapter 6 Power, politics and ideology

1. F. Parkin, *Class Inequality and Political Order,* MacGibbon and Kee, 1971.

2. S. Lukes, *Power: a radical view,* Macmillan, 1974.

3. E. Bott, *Family and Social Network,* Tavistock, 1957.

4. D. Lockwood, 'Sources of variation in working class images of society', *Sociological Review,* 14 (1966) 249.

5. J. H. Goldthorpe et al., 'Social stratification in industrial society', in

M. M. Tumin (ed.), *Readings on Social Stratification,* Prentice-Hall, 1970.

6. D. Lockwood, op. cit., 255.

7. See A. Fox and A. Flanders, 'The reform of collective bargaining: from Donovan to Durkheim', *British Journal of Industrial Relations,* 7 (1969) 151.

8. J. H. Goldthorpe, 'Social inequality and social integration in modern Britain', *Advancement of Science,* 26 (1969) 190.

9. K. Roberts et al., *The Fragmentary Class Structure,* Heinemann, 1977.

10. R. K. Brown and P. Brannen. 'Social relations and social perspectives amongst shipbuilding workers; a preliminary statement', *Sociology,* 4 (1970) 71 and 197.

11. R. Moore, *Pitmen, Preachers and Politics,* Cambridge University Press, 1974.

12. H. Newby, *The Deferential Worker,* Allen Lane, 1977; I. Carter, 'Agricultural workers in the class structure', *Sociological Review,* 22 (1974) 271.

13. E. Batstone, 'Deference and the ethos of small-town capitalism', in M. Bulmer (ed.), *Working Class Images of Society,* Routledge, 1976.

14. J. Platt, 'Variations in answer to different questions on perceptions of class', *Sociological Review,* 19 (1971) 409.

15. H. F. Moorhouse, 'Attitudes to class and class relations in Britain', *Sociology,* 10 (1976) 469.

16. R. Moore, op. cit.

17. A. Crosland, *The Future of Socialism,* Cape, 1956.

18. R. Dahrendorf, *Class and Class Conflict in Industrial Society,* Routledge, 1959.

19. A. M. Ross and P. T. Hartman, *Changing Patterns of Industrial Conflict,* Wiley, 1960.

20. G. K. Ingham, *Strikes and Industrial Conflict*, Macmillan, 1974.

21. D. Rose and D. Urwin, 'What are parties based on?', *New Society*, 7 May 1970.

22. W. E. J. McCarthy and S. Parker, *Shop Stewards and Workshop Relations*, Royal Commission on Trade Unions and Employers' Associations, Research Paper 10, HMSO, 1968.

23. S. Parker, *Workplace Industrial Relations*, HMSO, 1973.

24. J. Cousins, 'The non-militant shop steward', *New Society*, 3 February 1972.

25. See S. Wood and R. Elliott, 'A critical evaluation of Fox's radicalisation of industrial relations theory', *Sociology*, 11 (1977) 105.

26. J. A. Banks, *Marxist Sociology in Action*, Faber and Faber, 1970.

27. W. L. Guttsman, *The British Political Elite*, MacGibbon and Kee, 1963.

28. R. W. Johnson, 'The political elite', *New Society*, 24 Jan. 1974.

29. B. Hindess, *The Decline of Working Class Politics in Britain*, MacGibbon and Kee, 1971.

30. R. Michels, *Political Parties*, Dover Publications, 1959.

31. M. Warner, 'The big trade unions: militancy or maturity', *New Society*, 11 Dec. 1969; L. Donaldson and M. Warner, 'Bureaucratic and electoral control in occupational interest associations', *Sociology*, 8 (1974) 47.

32. W. L. Guttsman, *The English Ruling Class*, Weidenfeld and Nicholson, 1969.

33. J. Urry and J. Wakeford (eds), *Power in Britain*, Heinemann, 1973.

34. J. C. Kincaid, *Poverty and Equality in Britain*, Penguin, 1973.

35. Royal Commission on the Distribution of Income and Wealth, *Initial Report*, HMSO, 1975.

36. A. B. Atkinson, *Unequal Shares: Wealth in Britain*, Allen and Unwin, 1972

37. R. W. Jackman, 'Political democracy and social equality: a comparative analysis', *American Sociological Review*, 39, (1974) 29.

38. G. Polanyi and J. B. Wood, *How Much Inequality?*, Institute of Economic Affairs, Monograph 31, 1974.

39. F. Cairncross, 'Stark choice for the Unions', *The Guardian*, 2 Sept. 1974.

40. J. Foster, *Class Struggle and the Industrial Revolution*, Weidenfeld and Nicolson, 1974, p. 251.

41. H. F. Moorhouse, 'The political incorporation of the British working class', *Sociology*, 7 (1973) 341.

42. B. Jessop, *Traditionalism, Conservatism and British Political Culture*, Allen and Unwin, 1974.

43. For example, E. A. Nordlinger, *The Working Class Tories*, MacGibbon and Kee, 1967.

44. R. Q. Gray, 'The labour aristocracy in the Victorian class structure', in F. Parkin (ed), *The Social Analysis of Class Structure*, Tavistock, 1974.

45. R. Miliband, *The State in Capitalist Society*, Weidenfeld and Nicolson, 1969.

46. A. Fox, 'A social critique of pluralist ideology', in J. Child (ed), *Man and Organisation*, Allen and Unwin, 1973; A. Fox, *Beyond Contract*, Faber and Faber, 1974.

47. D. R. Webb, *Consensus and Ideology: a survey of social and political value systems*, M. A. thesis, University of Liverpool, 1971.

48. M. Mann, 'The social cohesion of liberal democracy', *American Sociological Review*, 35 (1970) 423.

49. R. Hyman, *Strikes*, Fontana, 1972; *Industrial Relations: a Marxist Introduction*, Macmillan, 1975.

50. L. Panitch, *Social Democracy and Industrial Militancy*, Cambridge University Press, 1976.

51. L. Minkin, 'The British Labour Party and the trade unions: crisis and compact', *Industrial and Labour Relations Review*, 28 (1974) 7.

52. M. Mann, *Consciousness and Action in the Western Working Class*, Macmillan, 1973.

53. T. Lane, *The Union makes us Strong*, Arrow, 1974.

54. R. Miliband, *Parliamentary Socialism*, Merlin Press, 1973.

55. This argument is developed in T. Nichols and P. Armstrong, *Workers Divided*, Fontana, 1976.

56. J. Westergaard and H. Resler, op. cit.

57. I. Meszaros, *Aspects of History and Class Consciousness*, Routledge, 1971.

58. H. Beynon, *Working for Ford*, Penguin, 1973.

59. R. Hyman, op cit.

60. V. Allen, *Militant Trade Unionism*, Merlin Press, 1966, *A Sociology of Industrial Relations*, Longman, 1971.

61. H. F. Moorhouse and C. W. Chamberlain, 'Lower class attitudes to property', *Sociology*, 8 (1974) 387; C. W. Chamberlain and H. F Moorhouse, 'Lower class attitudes towards the British political system', *Sociological Review*, 22 (1974) 503.

62. T Nichols and P. Armstrong, *Workers Divided*, Fontana, 1976.

63. R. M. Blackburn and M. Mann, 'Ideology in the non-skilled working class', in M. Bulmer (ed), *Working Class Images of Society* Routledge, 1976.

64. S. M. Elkins, *Slavery*, Chicago University Press, 1968.

65. E. Goffman, *Asylums*, Penguin, 1968.

66. F. Parkin, 'Working class conservatives: a theory of political deviance', *British Journal of Sociology*, 18 (1967) 278.

67. F. Parkin, *Class Inequality and Political Order,* op cit.

68. M. Stacey et al., *Power, Persistence and Change*, Routledge, 1975.

69. R. E. Dowse and J. Hughes, 'The family, the school and the political socialisation process', *Sociology*, 5 (1971) 21.

70. R. Stradling and E. Zurick, 'Political and non-political ideals of English primary and secondary schoolchildren', *Sociological Review*, 19 (1971) 203.

71. S. Cotgrove and C. Vamplew, 'Technology, class and politics; a study of process workers', *Sociology*, 6 (1972) 169.

Chapter 7 The working class in society and sociology

1. Including J. and E. Newson, *Infant Care in an Urban Community*, Allen and Unwin, 1963; and *Four Years Old in an Urban Community*, Allen and Unwin, 1968.

2. See M. Mann, *Workers on the Move*, Cambridge University Press, 1973, and K. Roberts et al., *The Fragmentary Class Structure*, Heinemann, 1977.

3. Ibid.

4. S. Parker, *Workplace Industrial Relations*, HMSO, 1973.

5. See K. Roberts, G. White and H. J. Parker, *The Character-Training Industry*, David and Charles, 1974.

6. K. Roberts et al., *The Fragmentary Class Structure*, Heinemann, 1977.

7. See R. K. Brown and P. Brannen, 'Social relations and social perspectives amongst shipbuilding workers: a preliminary statement', *Sociology*, 4 (1970) 71 and 197.

8. J. Platt, 'Variations in answer to different questions on perceptions of class', *Sociological Review*, 19 (1971) 409.

9. J. Cousins, 'The non-militant Shop Steward', *New Society*, 24 Jan. 1974.

10. R. M. Blackburn and M. Mann, 'Ideology in the non-skilled working class', in M. Bulmer (ed), *Working Class Images of Society*, Routledge, 1976.

11. T. Nichols and P. Armstrong, *Workers Divided*, Fontana, 1976.

12. T. Lane and K. Roberts, *Strike at Pilkingtons*, Fontana, 1971.

13. See Ibid.

14. A. Flanders et al., *Experiment in Industrial Democracy*, Faber, 1968.

15. F. Blum, *Work and Community*, Routledge, 1968.

16. See J. Gower Davies, *The Evangelistic Bureaucrat*, Tavistock, 1972.

17. K. Roberts et al., op cit.

Further reading

H. Beynon, *Working for Ford*, Penguin, 1973.

R. K. Brown and P. Brannen, 'Social relations and social perspectives amongst shipbuilding workers: a preliminary statement', *Sociology*, 4 (1970) 71 and 197.

M. Bulmer (ed), *Working Class Images of Society*, Routledge, 1975.

I. C. Cannon, 'Ideology and occupational community: a study of compositors', *Sociology*, 1 (1967) 165.

A. Fox, 'The meaning of work', in *Occupational Categories and Cultures, 1*. Open University Press, 1976.

J. H. Goldthorpe et al., *The Affluent Worker in the Class Structure*, Cambridge University Press, 1969.

R. Greenslade, *Goodbye to the Working Class*, Marion Boyars, 1976.

A. H. Halsey, 'Sociology and the equality debate', *Oxford Review of Education*, 1 (1975) 9.

B. Jackson, *Working Class Community*, Routledge, 1968.

M. L. Kohn, *Class and Conformity*, Dorsey Press, 1969.

D. Lockwood, 'Sources of variation in working class images of society', *Sociological Review*, 14 (1966) 249.

M. Mann, *Workers on the Move*, Cambridge University Press, 1973.

M. Mann, 'The social cohesion of liberal democracy', *American Sociological Review*, 35 (1970) 423.

M. Mann, *Consciousness and Action in the Western Working Class*, Macmillan, 1973.

R. Moore, *Pitmen, Preachers and Politics*, Cambridge University Press, 1974.

H. F. Moorhouse, 'The political incorporation of the British working class', *Sociology*, 7 (1973) 341.

H. F. Moorhouse, 'Attitudes to class and class relationships in Britain', *Sociology*, 10 (1976) 469.

H. Newby, *The Deferential Worker*, Allen Lane, 1977.

T. Nichols and P. Armstrong, *Workers Divided*, Fontana, 1976.

K. Roberts et al., *The Fragmentary Class Structure*, Heinemann, 1977.

J. Westergaard and H. Resler, *Class in a Capitalist Society*, Heinemann, 1975.

Index

The Working Class

Clausen, R., 35, 180, 181
Closed shop, 166
Coates, K., 68, 186
Cobb, J., 37, 182
Collective bargaining, 136–54
Collectivism, 141
Commodity consciousness, 62
Community, 72–80
Community, schools, 114–15, 176
Compensatory education, 121
Comprehensive schools, 104
Conflict theory, 1
Conservative Party, 9–10, 12–13,
    58–9, 142
Contraception, 84
Cook-Gumperz, J., 191
Corporatism, 146
Cotgrove, S., 43, 159, 183, 198
Council housing, 74–82, 91–2, 153,
    175
Cousins, J. M., 63, 141, 185, 195
Craft administration, 32
Craig, C., 30, 180
Crime, 94–7
Crompton, R., 43–4, 183
Crosland, A., 139, 194
Crowther Report, 110, 190
Cultural deprivation, 110–17,
    123–7, 176
Culture of poverty, 68
Curriculum, 124–5
Cycle of deprivation, 68–70

Dahrendorf, R., 139, 194
Dale, R., 192
Davie, R., 92, 188, 189
Davis, L. E., 182
Davis, R. L., 63, 185
Day-release, 176
Deference, 135–8, 148
Degradation theory, 44
Delinquency, 94–7
Dennis, N., 77, 186, 187
De-skilling, 44
Divorce, 96–7
Doeringer, P. B., 184, 186
Donaldson, L., 195

Douglas, J. W. B., 94, 126, 188, 189,
    190, 192, 193
Douvan, E. A., 189
Dowse, R. E., 158, 198
Dual labour market, 56
Dubin, R., 181
Duff, E., 180

Economic security, 26–30, 173–4
Education, 103–30, 158–9, 162,
    175–6
Educational Priority Areas, 114–17
Edwards, A. D., 121, 191
Eisenberg, L., 192
Elementary schools, 123–4
Eleven-plus, 104, 110
Elias, N., 96, 188
Elkins, S. M., 197
Elliot, R., 195
Embourgeoisement, 53–4, 58–64
Employment dependence, 43
Employment Protection Act 1975,
    27
Estates, 1
Ethnic minorities, 65–6, 77, 130
Eysenck, H. J., 190

Factory consciousness, 152
False consciousness, 133, 160, 161
Family, 72–102, 134
Farrington, D. P., 94, 188
Fatalism, 157
Fertility, 78, 83–4, 90
Field, F., 180
Finlayson, D., 113, 190
Flanders, A., 137, 194, 199
Ford, J., 95, 188, 189
Form, W. H., 55, 184
Foster, J., 147–8, 149, 196
Fox, A., 32, 33, 42, 137, 149, 181,
    182, 194, 196, 199
Friedman, W. L., 192
Friedmann, G., 181
Fringe benefits, 29–31, 48–9
Fryer, R. H., 28, 35, 180, 181
Functionalism, 1, 15–18, 39, 57–8,
    71, 102